Leadership Is A Choice

**Keep Your Fears From Holding You Back And
Make The Choice To Be A Leader**

**John DiCicco, Ph.D.
Kenneth E. Strong Jr., M.S.**

UNION SQUARE
PUBLISHING

Published by
Union Square Publishing 301 E. 57th Street, 4th floor
New York, NY 10022
www.unionsquarepublishing.com

Manufactured in the United States of America, or in the United Kingdom when distributed elsewhere.

DiCicco, John
Leadership is a Choice: Conquer Your Fears and Make the Decision to Lead
LCCN: 2017952809
ISBN: 978-1-946928-12-2
eBook: 978-1-946928-14-6

Cover design by: Joe Potter Interior design: Nathan Harmony

Photo credits: Gerry Evelyn / Evelyn Images

www.johndicicco.com

Dedication

To all the future leaders and the extraordinary people you will lead. And to all the extraordinary people I have led during the last thirty years. This book is dedicated to my first leader and mentor, my father, who showed me the way.

Kenneth E. Strong, Jr.
December 7, 2007 Virginia Beach, VA

I wish to recognize all those who make a difference through effective leadership at all levels. Years of experience have taught me that leaders are not born, but are developed as a result of their choices. I dedicate this book to my brother Ralph, a scholar, gentleman, soldier, friend and true leader in every sense of the word.

John A. DiCicco, Ph.D.
December 7, 2007 Brockton, MA

Kenneth E. Strong, Jr. M.S. holds a Master of Science in Health Care Administration from Salve Regina College and a Bachelor of Science in Health Services Administration from Providence College.

A health care executive for more than thirty years, he has had articles published by the American Geriatric Society and spoken on a variety of topics for the American College of Health Care Administrators and the New England Not-for- Profit Providers Conferences. He has also served as Adjunct Professor at Stonehill College.

Mr. Strong established the North Hill Academy, a corporate training center focused on leadership training for all levels of employees, the first of its kind in New England.

Mr. Strong was formerly the Leadership Development Specialist for the city of Virginia Beach where he designed and developed leadership programs for new supervisors and middle and upper managers based on the West Point Leadership Program.

A Certified Instructor in Achieve Global Leadership and Service courseware, Mr. Strong is also certified by the Center for Leadership Studies to teach Situational Leadership.

John A. DiCicco, Ph.D. has been President of Organizational Analysis Systems, a management consulting group, since 1991. OAS specializes in consulting and training upper and middle level managers to be more responsible leaders in both privately and publicly owned industries.

Dr. DiCicco is a member of Curry College's Department of Management in Milton, MA and holds the rank of Senior Lecturer, teaching Economics, Employment and Labor Law, Collective Bargaining, Business Ethics, Organizational Systems and Processes, Leadership, Human Resource Management, Personal Finance, International Business and Senior Seminar. He has also participated in the design and construction of a new MBA Degree Program in Leadership and Strategic Planning at Curry.

Dr. DiCicco holds a Ph.D. in Higher Education Administration and Professional Development from Capella University in Minneapolis, MN an M.S. in Applied Management and B.S. in Organizational Behavior from Lesley University's School of Management and an A.S. in Business Management from Fisher College, both in Boston, MA.

He is also Chair of Graduate Business and Management Programs at the University of Phoenix, Greater Massachusetts Campuses.

Table of Contents

What Others Are Saying About
Leadership Is A Choice

I read your book on my return plane trip from the West Coast. How enjoyable it was, just like reading a top novel, yet gaining great insight to the pros and cons of business leadership.

Hap Leven, Vice President-Sales, California Paint

The book offers a real scenario that I could relate to about a situation that we as leaders (or future leaders) could find ourselves in. I especially enjoyed the napkin theory and how it passed on particular and specific wisdom as it was needed, and challenged the character to think and explore its meaning, then apply it.

Patti Comeau, Executive Asst. HR., Reebok International

The book represents an outstanding learning experience for professionals at all levels and tells a compelling story at the same time. The offering balances lessons in leadership and management throughout and its interesting characters display a broad range of traits from humility to strategic thinking. A must read for all interested in building leadership skills.

Mark D. Sotir, Director of Customer Relations,
Barrett Distribution Center

The book epitomizes the meaning of an effective mentoring relationship and is easy to read because of the story format. I recommend this book to others and would be proud to add it to my library of leadership resources and tools.

Michelle L. Bleakley, Senior Manager, Provider Support,
Blue Cross Blue Shield of Massachusetts

The book is easy to read and unravels the complexities that a leadership role presents in a very sensible manner. This book sets itself above the rest and should be on the top shelf.

Joyce D. McCarthy, SPHR, HR Manager-Eastern Region,
Laidlaw Education Services, Inc.

Introduction

Every endeavor begins as a single thought followed by a conversation with close friends or in the privacy of your own mind. This book is no different.

John and I have met at a coffee shop every other Sunday morning for the past three years to discuss the world's events, our families and of course what's been happening at work.

We learned that we faced similar work issues and challenges. The more we talked about our situations the more apparent it became that perhaps others could benefit from our experiences and methods to resolve and or prevent leadership problems.

We concluded that the vast majority of problems in the workplace are the result of poor leadership skills. Today there is so much focus on finance, computer science, law, regulatory compliance, medicine and other so called hard skills that how we deal with the people we work with every day isn't given the significance it deserves.

How we relate to one another is more important than the hard skills. Without good people who are well trained and highly motivated nothing in the workplace will get done. It takes good leaders and good followers to make an organization successful. It also requires a good system, supported by top management, to identify and develop good leaders. To acknowledge the importance of the people you lead, we adopted the axiom, "Love your employees more than your customers."

We determined that the best way to teach our material was through the telling of a story. We wanted the teaching points to be practical and easy to apply on the job.

We wanted to make sure that a secondary learning style for our readers was part of this book. We both strongly believe that adults learn in a variety of ways. As a review for our readers, there are three major learning styles; visual, auditory and kinesics, non-verbal communication through body movements and gestures. Of course, many of us combine one or more of the three styles.

As a young man, I remember traveling with my father on his business trips and I often saw him make notes on a cocktail napkin. The napkin notes became the medium for our teaching points.

Following each chapter after chapter two, there is a graphic illustrating that chapter's theme and a brief exposition of each drawing's teaching point. Getting the most out of this book is simple.

1. Read each chapter through completely.
2. View the drawing at the end of each chapter for twenty seconds and read the accompanying discussion.
3. Reread the chapter and take notes about key learning points and capture ideas you want to apply on the job. Pages for your notes and action plans are included throughout the book.
4. Teach what you have learned in each chapter to someone else. Through the act of teaching the lessons in this book you will master its contents.

You have made the decision to become a leader. That decision makes you an extraordinary individual. Your leadership will make a unique contribution to your organization, your community and your family.

Lead by example. Set the standards high and always put the welfare of the people you lead ahead of yourself. As a leader you will be challenged beyond your abilities many times. Don't let that stop you; the rewards are well worth the effort.

You want to be the company's go to person; you want to be the person who gets the call when there is the greatest danger of failure or the absolute need to succeed. In the Army we had a saying that the best soldiers get the worst assignments. That statement is just as true in the corporate world.

You will be given assignments that no one wants or has the courage to take on. You will be criticized by your peers for becoming a leader and perhaps for making them look bad. At times you will be lonely because your decisions may be unpopular or require additional effort by others to accomplish the task.

You will spend time gathering information and data from as many individuals and experts on a given subject as possible. Remember people support best what they help to create. In the end you will make the decision alone when you have 70% of the information. Learn to be your own best company. You and you alone make the decision.

The rewards of leadership are numerous. A few examples are getting recognition from superiors and subordinates, seeing people grow and develop new skills and confidence, leading people from the unknown to the known, developing new programs or sources of revenue, modernizing an outdated process or improving employee morale.

Receiving a raise or promotion and the satisfaction of a job well done, though welcome rewards, are not always the most significant ones.

Some rewards you will never know until after you leave the job. Here is an example. Shortly after leaving my last position of eighteen years, I began receiving letters from former employees.

The letters were in the form of a recommendation to a future employer. Their letters talked about what they had learned from me; how they accomplished things they never thought possible because of my encouragement and support and how they felt about me as a person, not as a boss.

That type of reward cannot be measured in dollars. It just demonstrates that as a leader you may never know what kind of impact you will have on the people you lead. So make sure that it will always be a positive one.

The leadership skills you are about to learn are proven to work effectively if you consistently practice them. John and I have used them successfully in our business lives and you can too.

Yours in Leadership Success,

Ken and John

Chapter One

The Journey Begins

My name is Mike Berber and my story began about a year ago. No, I guess it really began long before that but the trauma that set me on the journey I want to tell you about began about a year ago. Trauma sounds pretty dramatic, but it's been defined as something that jars the mind or emotions, and it certainly did both to me.

I was a data base administrator with about a dozen bosses, but it didn't matter. I knew my job, the bosses knew me, and every day I went to work and did the same thing. They were satisfied and I was satisfied. Sure it was same old, same old, but there was no pressure, no unknowns and it was secure.

And then a British firm bought out the company and the layoffs began. I was one of the first to go! I couldn't believe it. I had been with the company much longer than some in the same position who weren't laid off. To make bad matters even worse, the job market was very tight at that time and I couldn't find work.

My severance pay and unemployment ran out after 18 months and I still had no job in sight. My wife had taken a secretarial job working school hours, but we had three young children and were rapidly depleting our meager savings. Bills were going unpaid, creditors were calling us daily and we were even in danger of losing our house. I was getting desperate for a job. I was going on three or four interviews a week and applying to about a dozen places every day with no success. In my interviews everyone seemed to be looking for someone with supervisory experience, someone who wanted to be a leader.

John A. DiCicco and Kenneth E. Strong, Jr.

I used to be a leader; in fact it was my job to teach men and women to be leaders. That was when I was a drill instructor in the Army. I always got superior scores in my annual reviews. I even had several letters of commendation from superior officers, but that was then and this is now.

When I left the service I went back to school to get training for a stable civilian career. It was a big change from the army, but I wanted to settle down, get married and have a family. I wanted a job that was steady and secure, one where I wouldn't be moving my family from place to place all the time.

About four years ago, after responding to countless newspaper ads and going on job interviews where I didn't get the job, I finally got a job as a data base administrator at Crown Company. My salary at Crown was less than it had been with my former company, but it was still an employer's market and this was better than no job at all.

My boss, Joe Berringer, Director of the Information Technology Department at Crown, is resigning in three months to take a position with the federal government. The company is looking for his replacement in house and his position pays a great deal more than I made with my old company. I've thought about applying for Joe's position. I certainly have all the technical skills that are needed, but I am a little leery of the responsibilities that I don't have in my present job.

Even if I could get the job, I don't know if I want the responsibility of directing the work of 20 people. They would all report directly to me and I would be responsible for their performances as well as my own. The bigger salary would be great, but I'd sure earn it, being responsible for 20 people. I've become pretty comfortable in my current position and I'm leaning toward just leaving well enough alone.

It's funny in a way that years ago I could turn more than 100 raw recruits into leaders who got things done and now I'm afraid to supervise 20 experienced people. Well I'm not afraid really; I'm just being realistic. I need to stay focused on doing my own job.

I'm very good at what I do and I need very little direction to do my job well. It is much safer to get direction than to give it. Who knows how long it would take me to find another job if I lost this one. I don't want to become unemployed again,ever!

The deadline is coming up to let human resources know if I'm interested in Joe's job and I think I've just about made up my mind to stay right where I am. It's better to be safe than sorry. I'll explain it to my wife, Alice, at dinner tonight. She knows I've become comfortable in the job I have and I know she'll support my decision just as she has throughout our marriage.

When I got home Alice had dinner ready, the children greeted me enthusiastically, and after the usual hugs and kisses we sat down to dinner. At the dinner table we always talk about upcoming events and what went on in our respective days.

When it was my turn I started to talk about the director's position that would soon be open and before I could finish the sentence, Alice interrupted by asking, "You are going to apply for the job, aren't you? Didn't you say that there is a deadline to indicate whether or not you are interested?"

I paused before answering, directing my full attention on cutting my steak, and without looking up at Alice, said, "I haven't decided yet whether I want the job or not."

When I finally looked up at her, she was wearing her raised eyebrows look, which I knew meant, "*What* did you say?"

My response to Alice's question wasn't received as I thought it would be. The children became silent, which was unusual for them, and Alice was still wearing her raised eyebrows look. I was embarrassed and I excused myself and went into the family room.

A short time later Alice came in and asked if I was okay. I just smiled at her and told her I was fine. She said, "Dessert is ready.

Don't you want to come back to the table and have some?"

I shook my head and said, "No thanks, I really don't want any dessert." She patted me softly on the shoulder and went back to the kitchen.

I began to read the newspaper to try to relax. I paged through the paper, going through the motions of looking for something of interest, but I had trouble concentrating on what I was reading. When I finally put the paper down I realized I had no idea at all what I had just read.

I began to feel very peculiar. There seemed to be tightness in my chest and I was having trouble breathing. Alice came into the room, took one look at me and ran to the phone to call 911.

The paramedics arrived in less than ten minutes, put an oxygen mask on my face, started an IV and rushed me to the hospital. Five hours later Alice and I were talking to the cardiologist. He informed us that all tests confirmed that my heart was fine and I had not had a heart attack.

Alice said, "That's wonderful news, Doctor, but something had to cause this."

The doctor asked me if these episodes happened often and I told him that I had never before experienced anything like this. He said he thought I was suffering from acute anxiety and had had a panic attack. He asked if I was experiencing any unusual stress lately and I said I couldn't think of any. I didn't feel comfortable telling the doctor what was causing my stress. I wasn't even comfortable admitting to myself what was causing it.

Then Alice asked him if it could be defined as stress if one were experiencing some sort of inner conflict, sort of an argument with oneself. He said it certainly could and that stress can be internal as well as external.

Alice's question surprised me, but I didn't comment. The

doctor gave me a prescription for a mild sedative and told me to follow up with my primary care physician.

The ride home from the hospital was a silent one. The children had fallen asleep in the back of the van and Alice was driving. I felt both relieved and embarrassed. Alice went into the drugstore to get my prescription filled, and I sat in the car feeling foolish.

After we got home and the children had been put to bed, Alice and I sat down in the kitchen and with tears trickling down her cheeks, she said she had never been so frightened in her life, because she thought she was going to lose me.

After she had a good cry I explained to her that I was really conflicted about applying for the director's position and that is what caused the panic attack. I wanted to reassure her that there was nothing wrong with my health. Her response was not at all what I expected.

"Is that what this was all about?" she asked in icy tones. "You exhibited all the symptoms of a heart attack because you are afraid of being considered for a promotion? Your internal conflict is simply indecision?

"I was afraid that you had some health problem you wouldn't admit to. Whether you do or don't want this job will have no effect whatever on our relationship. If it makes you happy and is really what you want, you can stay in the job you have for the rest of your working life and that will be fine with me."

She took a deep breath, and in her usual tone, added, "But if you would really like to have that job you need to figure out why you're afraid to go after it and resolve the conflicted feelings that brought on that panic attack.

"I know you could do that job, Mike, and do it very well, but only you can decide if you want to do it. I'm going to check on the children now and then I'm going to bed. It's been a very long night." And with that she left the room.

I was stunned at Alice's comments. At the hospital when she asked about internal conflict I thought she must have had a pretty good idea about what brought the attack on. Apparently it had never occurred to her that it was my indecision about the job. And on what does she base her conviction that I can do Joe's job?

As I was having these thoughts, I looked at the wall in front of me, where I had an array of pictures, letters and certificates from my service days. The man I was then wouldn't think much of the man I am now. But the man I was then didn't have a family to take care of.

Still I couldn't stop thinking about that panic attack. A panic attack caused by indecision. And indecision caused by what? Lack of confidence? Why has my confidence diminished to the point that I hesitate to try to move ahead in my career? Fear of responsibility? Fear of accountability? Fear of unemployment? Yes, I do fear that. That's why I just want to do the job I know and not take any unnecessary chances.

Chapter Two

No People, No Mission, No Margin

I arrived at work the next day and did what I do every day. I went to my computer, checked my E-mail messages, got my coffee and began my usual routine. It's very predictable and some days it verges on boring, but I get a regular paycheck and as long as I do my job I'm in no jeopardy of losing it.

Yet for some reason I kept thinking about that director's position. It would involve a major change in my responsibilities and I'd certainly have to put more time in on the job. And the more responsibility you have, the more accountability you have. The nail that sticks up is the one that gets hit. Why was I even thinking about taking a risk I didn't need to take?

Even though Alice thought I should go for the job I knew she would be supportive of my decision, whatever it was. I was trying to be honest with myself, as she had asked me to be, about why I might not want the job.

I was finding that being honest with myself was more difficult than being honest with anyone else. I scowled at my cup of coffee and decided that it tasted bitter, so I went to the cafeteria to get a freshly brewed cup.

When I got to the cafeteria I saw Russ Jacobs, Crown's CEO. He was the Chief Operating Officer when I was hired, but shortly after I joined the company he became the CEO. As my coffee brewed I glanced around the room and made eye contact with Russ, who waved me over to his table.

He gestured for me to sit in the chair opposite him and asked,

"Mike, did you know that Crown's stock has risen 11 points over the past year?"

I replied that I didn't know that, and then thought to myself that it was something I probably should have known.

Then he said, "Mike, I selected some personnel files to review last week, and in looking through yours I refreshed my memory about your excellent record in the Army. You must be very proud of that."

"Yes I am," I replied. "I don't mean to sound boastful, but I know I made a positive difference in the lives of a lot of young men and women."

"I'm sure you did," Russ said, nodding his head. "You made leaders out of many of those young soldiers, didn't you?"

"Most of them," I replied, surprising myself at speaking out that way. "But that was my job," I added, hoping to soften what might have sounded too much like blowing my own horn.

"Didn't you have to be a leader to accomplish what you did with those young people?" Russ asked.

"Of course," I answered, "But that was part of the job."

"Tell me, Mike," he said, looking at me intently, "Do you think there is such a thing as a born leader?"

"No I don't," I answered without hesitation. "My experience in the military showed me that leaders are made, not born. I trained a lot of soldiers to be leaders who certainly weren't born that way."

After a slight pause Russ said with the hint of a smile, "That's a very perceptive answer."

Even though he was fully engaged in our conversation, I noticed that while we were talking he was doing some sort of sketch and writing something on a paper napkin.

I glanced at my watch and saw it was well past lunch time, so I said, "I really have to get back to work, Russ but I've enjoyed talking with you."

He finished whatever he was writing on the napkin and said, "I've enjoyed it too, Mike. And I'd like to do it again. In the meantime, here's something I'd like you to look at and think about," and he handed me the napkin. "I mean really think about it, Mike, before we talk again."

I thanked him, took the napkin and went back to my desk. When I got there I put the napkin down on a stack of papers and got to work. I did the usual day's work, but I couldn't get that talk with Russ off my mind. I wondered why he had made a point of talking to me and why he had been reviewing personnel files.

Of course I was most interested in why my file was one of those he selected. And why does he want to talk to me again? If he was trying to find out if I'm interested in the director's position, why didn't he just ask me?

It wasn't until the end of the day that I remembered about the napkin. I picked it up and looked at it. It was a sketch of a cube with these words inside the cube:

No People—No Mission—No Margin

And beneath that was a thought provoking quotation. I thought about Russ's napkin note all the way home from work. I was so deep in thought I almost missed the turn onto our street. A part of me wanted to dismiss the whole conversation with Russ and his sudden interest in me. But another part of me was flattered by it. He must at least think I'm worth his time. And it would be logical for me to be interested in Joe's job.

Although it would have been much simpler for him to come right out with whatever point he was trying to make, he must have a reason for the approach he was taking. The man was the CEO of the company after all and I didn't think he was just playing head games with me. He never seemed like that kind of a guy. Maybe Joe's job had nothing to do with it, and Russ was taking an interest in me for some other reason. But I couldn't imagine what that could be.

I pulled in the driveway and turned the engine off and just sat there, thinking about No People, No Mission, No Margin, and that quotation.

I heard Alice's voice, looked up and saw her standing by the car window, wearing a concerned expression.

"Are you all right?" she asked. "You've been sitting in the driveway for five minutes."

"Oh, I'm fine, Alice, I was just thinking about something that happened at work today. I'd like to talk to you about it after we put the kids to bed."

"You certainly were deep in thought. And it must be something good because you seem sort of energized."

"Yes, I guess I am, sort of, but let's talk about it later."

We had dinner, tucked the kids in after the usual struggle and Alice and I went to the family room.

"Alright," Alice said, what's the big mystery?"

I told her about seeing Russ in the cafeteria and repeated our conversation.

"He was the one who hired me," I reminded her. "Of course he was the Chief Operating Officer when I was hired, but he became the CEO a short time later."

"Yes, I remember. But what was on the napkin he gave you?"

I took the napkin out of my pocket and handed it to Alice.

"No People, No Mission, No Margin," she read. "What does that mean?"

"That was my first reaction, but read the quotation. Read it out loud."

Alice read, " This was said by Edward Paul Abbey, '*In social institutions, the whole is always less than the sum of its parts. There will never be a state as good as its people, or a church worthy of itscongregation, or a university equal to its faculty and students.*' That makes it a lot clearer for me."

"What do you think it means, Alice?"

"I think it means whether it's the state or a church, a university or whatever, people are what matter most."

"Yes, I think that's the gist of it. And your whatever would include a company. And if the company didn't have good people it wouldn't be able to carry out its mission and there would be no margin."

"By margin you mean profit, don't you, Mike?"

"Exactly. But where do I fit in with all that?"

"Well, Mike, you are a person, aren't you?"

"Yes, I believe I qualify. But why me? Why has Russ singled me out for this attention?"

"You said that he seemed interested in your leadership role as a drill instructor."

"That was a long time ago, Alice."

"I'm sure Russ Jacobs is aware of that."

"Alice, do you think he's sizing me up for Joe's job?"

"That would be my guess. And maybe you're not the only person in the company he's talking to in the interest of sizing them up as you put it."

"But why is he going about this in such an indirect way?"

"I'm sure he has his reasons, Mike. He is the CEO and he must have a lot of demands on his time, so I don't think he's doing this without a good reason. But if you're not interested in the job you really ought to let him know."

"Are you using reverse psychology on me, Alice?"

"No, I'm not. It's just that now you appear to be interested in the job and it will probably seem that way to Mr. Jacobs, so if you really aren't interested you should let him know, that's all I'm saying."

"You're right, if I don't really want the job I shouldn't waste his time. But I do want to meet with him again and see how that goes."

"I just hope there aren't too many people on his sizing up list."

"Why, Alice, don't you think I could cut it with the competition?"

"Not at all Mike, I just don't want him to run out of napkins."

No People—No Mission—No Margin

In social institutions, the whole is always less than the sum of its parts. There will never be a state as good as its people, or a church worthy of its congregation, or a university equal to its faculty and students.

Edward Paul Abbey

It is easy to forget that the people performing the task or service are the critical components of a business and your success as a manager. Technology improves our everyday life, bringing with it new methods of efficient delivery of a product or service. We are in awe of what technology can do. There are many benefits of technology but none of them can replace the human contributions to the success of the organization.

You've heard the statement the customer is always right. Customers have a right to their view; to receive a product or service equal to the value they paid for it, the fulfillment of a guarantee, resolution of a complaint and your undivided attention. But the customer is not always right.

There is no excuse for inappropriate behavior on the part of the customer and it is not part of your job to dutifully accept the customer's inappropriate behavior. This applies equally to internal and external customers.

As a leader it is your responsibility to intervene with an inappropriate customer. If you don't defend your employees you won't keep them very long to provide exceptional service to customers. Your competition will be happy to hire your experienced employees.

You may have the finest product or service in the world but without quality employees to deliver the product or service no one will care and you won't be in business.

Of course all customers are important; getting and keeping good customers is expensive and their purchases are the life-blood of a company. But it is better for you to lose an inappropriately behaving customer than a valued staff member by not defending your employee.

Here is a simple rule for keeping good employees. When things do not go well, you as the manager take the blame or responsibility and when things do go well you give all the credit to the employee.

If you follow this rule faithfully you will have the most loyal group of employees imaginable, who will do anything for you as long as it is not unethical, unlawful or immoral.

All endeavors begin as a single thought about what you want to do or become. In the military or in business it is called the mission. In our daily life it is called an objective. No mission can be accomplished without the efforts and sacrifices of people.

Your idea or dream will never become a reality without the labors of the individual. If you want to accomplish your mission or objective you must put your employees first and the customer second. Remember all that you are is the result of someone else's sacrifice.

No business or household will function very long without margin, the excess of revenues over expenses. A business, department, team or household can be a very complex operation and must have a variety of elements such as a business, marketing, and strategic plan to guide its development and daily operational objective.

Assuming that you have all the elements in place, a marketable product or service to sell, nothing will happen without good people and a good mission. These statements are an over simplification but nonetheless valid.

Remember:

No People—No Mission—No Margin

Chapter Three

Three Building Blocks Of Leadership

The next day I went to work a little earlier than usual. I didn't even know whether I would have an opportunity to talk to Russ that day or not, but I thought I might and I was just eager to get to the office and try to resolve my indecision.

I kept turning over in my mind the talk I had with Alice last night. When it got to be lunchtime I began to feel apprehensive. What if Russ was sizing me up for the director's job?

What if he wanted me to get the job and I didn't really want it? That would be a sure way to lessen myself in his eyes. And if I did say I wanted the job and didn't get it that would lessen me in my own eyes.

"Mike, I have an important project for you."

I glanced up and saw my boss, Joe Berringer, standing in the doorway holding a sheaf of papers.

I offered Joe a cup of coffee and suggested that we sit at the table. What followed was an intense briefing about the project Joe had for me.

"Mike, we need extensive marketing and production data to be used in a critical presentation for a very important prospective client. We could become the leading company in our industry if we are successful in winning this client."

"When do you want this, Joe?"

"I want it yesterday, but I need it ASAP. It has to be complete, right the first time and as easy to understand as you can possibly make it. I want to be fully briefed in all the technical aspects of this in preparation for mypresentation."

Joe briefed me for about thirty minutes, emphasizing repeatedly how important it was that the data be complete, correct and easy to understand and explain. Joe's people skills are much better than his technical skills and it was pretty clear that he was really anxious about his ability to make the technical aspects clear.

As he was leaving, he said, "I can't stress enough the urgency and importance of this, Mike. I'm really counting on you."

"I understand, Joe, and I'll get you what you need when you need it, no problem." That brought the first hint of a smile to Joe's face since he came into the office.

"Good, Mike, that's a big relief. Now I'll just get out of here so you can get to work."

I wasn't so sure that Joe had reason to feel relieved. It would be a time consuming project, but I was confident that I could get it done on time and have it complete and correct. But I was not as confident that I could make it as easy to understand as Joe needed it to be. But I'd sure give it my best shot.

I glanced at the clock and saw that it was time to go to the cafeteria.

I got my lunch, found an empty table facing the door and hoped no one other than Russ would join me. When I was almost finished with my lunch he walked in, came straight to my table, sat down, and asked, "What did you think of my message?"

"It really made me think, Russ."

"Made you think what, Mike?"

"That maybe you want me to apply for the supervisor's position."

Russ said nothing and just looked at me as though he was waiting for me to say more.

Finally he broke the silence by saying, "And?"

"And I wondered, why me?"

"Why not you, Mike?"

"I'm just not sure I'm cut out for that job."

"What do you want, Mike, a guarantee? No one ever really knows if they can do a job until they do it. No one is cut out for a given job; they grow into it. It's as you said about leaders, they are made, not born. Tell me what you got from my message, Mike. Exactly what did it mean to you?"

"That your people are of supreme importance. Without them you have no mission and no margin," I said.

"Mike, every company has people. That seems like a rather simplistic interpretation. Can't you amplify that?" Russ asked.

"It means that you have to nurture and train your people, you have to let them know how special they are. You have to show them you appreciate them and help them be the best they can be so the company retains them and they and the company grow."

"Exactly, Mike. And as CEO of this company it is my role to find and develop good, talented people, by giving them all the authority, responsibility and accountability they need to get the successful results the company needs.Seventy percent of my job is to find and continue to develop good talent or else we are out of business.

"Good talent can only flourish when your people are given all the authority needed to fulfill their responsibilities and the accountability for the results. You have to give your people the freedom to be innovative and to react to the unexpected without going through an onerous chain of command."

He paused to see if this was sinking in and then added, "You see, Mike, I believe people know what the right answer is, but they are often reluctant to implement the right decision, simply out of fear."

Now Russ was increasing my indecision, not helping resolve it, and in frustration I asked, "What do you want from me?"

He shook his head from side to side and said, "I want nothing from you. What do you want from you? As little as you can get away with, or all you can be?"

That really made me mad, and I said, "I do my job, Russ!"

"Sure," Russ said, "You do the job you have very well, but is that all you really want to do? Is it the most you're capable of? Give that question some serious thought, Mike. If you really aren't interested in doing anything more than your current job, we'll just drop this.

"But if you want to talk again, meet me back here next week at the same time. And in the meantime, give this some thought," Russ said, as he handed me a folded napkin, got up and left.

I couldn't have said at that moment whether I was relieved that Russ wanted to talk to me again or disappointed in myself that I hadn't just put an end to it by saying I wasn't interested in the job.

I didn't think his comment about people knowing the right answer but being afraid to implement a decision was a generalization. I thought it was meant for me. And that really got under my skin.

I went back to my desk, unfolded the napkin and saw a sketch of three ascending pillars with blocks sitting on top of each pillar, labeled:

Authority
Responsibility
Accountability

And there was another quotation, this one from W. W. Broadbent, M.D., Ph.D.:

"The major way of doing anything with one's self is to own one's self. This means to take full responsibility and accountability for whatever I am doing at any moment, with anybody. It means, among other things, that I get rid of all the extra fingers that I point at people and situations to explain my behavior. When a person says 'He made me mad,' that is not accurate. It is 'I made me mad.' When I permit myself the luxury of taking that full responsibility, then I'm on first base, at least, because then I can do something about it."

That really hit home. Did Russ make me mad with his comments, or did I make me mad because what he said about fear really applied to me?"

I wanted to talk to Alice about all this, but I knew I wouldn't say much to her about my latest talk with Russ. Before I talked to her again about anything having to do with the job opening I had to decide whether or not I wanted to apply for it. And if I didn't want to I needed to have a valid reason. Not just for Alice, but for me.

Three Building Blocks Of Leadership

23

It's not enough to declare that your selected candidate for promotion to supervisor is now a "leader." You must provide him or her with three essential building blocks. And by the way, if you are the one being asked to take on the additional responsibility of leadership you should insist on having the same three building blocks:

Authority

After this time I surpassed all others in authority,
but I had no more power than the others
who were also my colleagues in office.
Augustus Caesar

Authority includes the personnel, money and materials that go beyond the title supervisor or manager. Your authority includes the sole determination of how the above assets are utilized or expended conducting the business of your department, section, area of responsibility or company. Your staff must know that you are in charge and be absolutely certain that your decisions won't be reversed by your supervisor, within reason, barring anything unethical, unlawful or immoral.

If you aren't given the decision-making authority, don't take the job. Having the authority to complete a job is very satisfying. Remember that your authority also means taking responsibility when things go wrong. You are given the authority to perform your duties and responsibilities because of your supervisor's confidence and trust in your abilities.

Responsibility

While an open mind is priceless, it is priceless only when its owner has the courage to make a final decision that closes the mind for action after the process of viewing all sides of the question has been completed. Failure to make a decision after due consideration of all the facts will quickly brand a man as unfit for a position of responsibility. Not all of your decisions will be correct. None of us is perfect. But if you get into the habit of making decisions, experience will develop your judgment to a point where more and more of your decisions will be right. After all, it is better to be right 51% of the time and get something done, than it is to get nothing done because you fear to reach a decision.

H. W. Andrews

This is the lonely part of leadership; every decision you make you make alone. Of course you want to have input from staff members and others as may be necessary and you will evaluate all the data and advice and ultimately make the decision alone. Leaders are responsible for making the hard decisions no one else wants to make or can make.

Once you implement your decision everyone suddenly knows the correct answer. You have now opened yourself to criticism from every possible direction. You may even begin to second-guess yourself. Don't. The decision you made was based on available information and in the best interests of the organization.

Besides you always have the option of adjusting the decision as its consequences develop. As a leader you make decisions knowing that they may be wrong but you take that risk where others won't. You and you alone have the responsibility for making the decision. So make your decision with confidence and above all trust yourself.

Accountability

The major way of doing anything with one's self is to own one's self. This means to take full responsibility and accountability for whatever I am doing at any moment, with anybody. It means, among other things, that I get rid of all the extra fingers that I point at people and situations to explain my behavior. When a person says "He made me mad" that is not accurate. It is "I made me mad." When I permit myself the luxury of taking that full responsibility, then I'm on first base, at least, because then I can do something about it.

W. W. Broadbent, M.D., PhD

Accountability simply put means you own it.

The military teaches this concept better that any organization I know. It works like this. You are assigned a task; there are two possible outcomes; you succeed or you fail. If you succeed, congratulations and move on. If you fail, there is no excuse for failing; you just didn't get it done.

This short conversation sounds like this; Yes, Sir, No, Sir and No Excuse, Sir. The young leader learns very quickly that he or she is totally accountable for everything his or her unit does or fails to do. I guarantee you will only make an excuse once.

Your reputation as a leader will be determined by how accountable you are in your daily business practices. By holding yourself accountable for all your actions and those of your department you will be way ahead of your contemporaries. It is an easy way to get noticed in a positive way.

Accountability is not just for the big stuff; it is also important for the casual daily things. For example: You tell a colleague that you can't meet with him at the moment but will call him in an hour. Make sure you call him in an hour. Or you are scheduled to attend a meeting at 10:00 AM. Show up at 9:55 AM, not 10:05 AM.

Chapter Four

The Leadership Bridge

The next morning at work I had no pressing deadlines to divert my thoughts from the director's position. I knew Russ was out of town and I wouldn't see him until next week. That was really a relief because I was no closer to a decision than I had been yesterday. I wasn't even any closer to understanding why I found it so difficult to make a decision.

Was I hiding from the reason? Was I afraid of applying for the job? What was the worst thing that could happen? I wouldn't get the job. I'd still have a job. Was I willing to pass up an opportunity rather than take the chance that I wouldn't get the promotion?

I didn't want to think that about myself, but it sure fit. And why was Russ taking so much interest in me when I hadn't even committed to applying for the position? Did he see something in me I didn't see in myself? And if that is the case, what is in it for him?

Could it be that he sees himself as some kind of magician who can turn people into what he wants them to be? And why would he want to? Is this all a game to him?

And what was Russ's point in giving me that quotation about taking responsibility and accountability and not pointing fingers? I guess he is suggesting that I take the responsibility and accountability for making a decision about this job.

But the finger pointing doesn't apply. Unless he means that I'm using my family as an excuse not to take a chance. Thinking about this was just producing more questions and no answers and I was pleasantly surprised to see it was time to go to lunch.

Bernie, the director of financial services, was in line behind me in the cafeteria, and struck up a conversation. Bernie has been with Crown so long he is practically a fixture. He's not much of a talker, or at least I'd never had what you could call a real conversation with him.

When our paths crossed he would smile at me or give me the thumbs up sign of encouragement. I never heard anyone ever say anything negative about Bernie and I don't ever remember him taking a day off.

We exchanged trivialities about the menu and then he asked, "You applying for that supervisor's position in your department?"

I looked at him in surprise and said, "Why would you think I was?"

He smiled and asked, "Why wouldn't you?"

Since I didn't have the answer to that question I became very preoccupied with choosing my lunch. As I headed for an empty table Bernie followed me and asked, "Do you mind if I join you, or did you want to be alone?"

I said I'd be glad to have him join me and we took chairs opposite one another.

We talked about Crown and my jobs before Crown and I learned that Bernie started at Crown in the mailroom when he was 16. He just completed his 25th year with the company and as the director of his department he manages a staff of 14 employees.

When there was a lull in the conversation, I asked him, "Why did you say, why wouldn't you?"

He looked puzzled and said, "You just lost me, Mike."

"Bernie, when I asked you why you thought I was going to apply for the supervisor's job, you said, "Why wouldn't you?"

Bernie said, "Well, why wouldn't you?" "Come on, "Bernie, that's not an answer, that's a question and I really would like an answer."

"It wasn't an accusation," Bernie said. 'It was just a rhetorical question. It seemed like a logical assumption to me. You've been here long enough to be eligible to apply and I have noticed you spending a lot of time with Russ during lunch, so I made an assumption."

He leaned across the table toward me, looked me straight in the eye and said, "I answered your question, Mike, now you answer mine. Why wouldn't you?"

I was silent for a moment, then shook my head and said, "I don't know, Bernie, I really don't."

Bernie paused before he answered, "Russ doesn't take a special interest in an employee unless he thinks he or she is worth it. He is always on the lookout for people who can balance the needs of the company. He isn't looking for a specific personality or individual, he is looking for the skills the company needs or will need in the future. He must see something inyou."

I didn't reply to that, and I must have looked as confused as I felt. Bernie leaned toward me and spoke so softly, I had to lean toward him to hear what he was saying.

"I know the drill, Mike, at first you probably thought he was playing head games with you, but he doesn't do that. Russ is always on the lookout for people who can make a significant contribution to this company, people who can be leaders. I owe a lot to him. I wouldn't be where I am if it weren't for him."

We both sat back in our chairs and were silent for a moment. Then I said, "Bernie, I appreciate you telling me this, and assuming he does see something in me I don't see in myself, why is he going about it this way? Why not just sit down with me and tell me?"

Bernie shrugged and said, "I don't know. Maybe he wants you to see for yourself what he sees in you, to want it enough to figure it out for yourself. But I do know that if he is taking an interest in you it isn't about you, personally, it's about what he thinks you can contribute to the company.

"His approach to mentoring may be somewhat unusual but Russ doesn't do anything that isn't in the best interest of this company. He is not a capricious man. There is nothing arbitrary or random about anything he does."

Then Bernie stood up and said, "I tend to think you may have been exposed to Russ's penchant for quotations. He confided in me once that he learned the value of quotations very early in his career, when he had the good fortune to be mentored by a man who used them much as Russ does.

"One of my favorites is by Marian Anderson: 'Leadership should be born out of the understanding of the needs of those who would be affected by it.' We never had this conversation, Mike, but if we had my parting line would be, And why wouldn't you?" And with that he gave me the thumbs up and walked out of the cafeteria.

As I walked back to my office I thought about my resolution not to talk to Alice about the job opening until I had made my decision and could justify it, not as much to Alice as to myself. I realized, after my conversation with Bernie, that I needed to talk to Alice about it. Maybe I just needed to voice my thoughts. She has always been my sounding board and right now I needed every resource available tome.

That evening after dinner I broached the subject by telling Alice I had an interesting conversation with a coworker at lunch.

She said, "Something about the job opening, I assume."
"Why would you assume that?" I asked her.

"Because, Mike," she said with a smile, "that's been on your mind and mine since the night you went to the hospital. I assumed you didn't talk about it at breakfast because of the children."

"It wasn't just that, Alice. I didn't want to talk about it again until I had made up my mind," I said with a shrug.

"But I gather that shrug means you still haven't made up your mind."

"No, I haven't. But let me tell you about my conversation with Bernie today."

"Isn't Bernie the head of financial services, who has been there for over twenty years?"

"When did I ever mention Bernie? I never even had a real conversation with him until today."

"You never did mention him. I talked to him at the company picnic. He's an interesting guy. He comes from a family of eight. There was no way for his family to help him through college and he worked his way through, at Crown. He thinks very highly of the company and its CEO.

"Alice, you amaze me. You learned more about someone I work with in one afternoon that I have in all the time I've worked there. How did you do that?"

"It wasn't difficult; we just had a pleasant conversation and we talked about our families and our work. We all like to talk about ourselves when someone shows an interest. But tell me about your conversation with Bernie."

I told Alice what had taken place at lunchtime, almost word for word. When I finished she didn't say anything; she just looked at me with that questioning, raised eyebrows look. I finally said, "Well what is your reaction to all that?"

To take a page out of Bernie's book, "Why wouldn't you?"

"I'm getting awfully tired of that question, Alice," I said rather testily.

"There's an easy way to put an end to it, Mike. Just come up with an answer."

"That's easy for you to say."

"And it should be easy for you to say. Didn't you listen to Bernie? I mean really listen to him? He reinforced all the things Russ has been trying to make yousee."

"And what's that?"

"Oh, Mike," Alice said impatiently, "Maybe you shouldn't have talked to me about this until you made a decision."

"Alice, you've always been my sounding board, and I really need you to play that role now."

Alice took a deep breath and then said, "Okay, this is how I see it. Russ has been taking a lot of interest in you, encouraging you to apply for the director's job and letting you know he thinks you are leadership material. Why do you think he is doing that?"

"That's just it. I don't know. Is he playing head games with me? Or is it a power or control thing? Why me, that's what I keep asking myself."

"Why not you, Mike? Bernie is an intelligent man who has had a long time to observe Russ. From his personal experience and what he has seen in the company over his years of service he sees Russ as an ethical, responsible, savvy CEO whose sole interest is in finding the necessary talent the company needs to stay strong.

"I doubt that Bernie is the only employee he has ever mentored. And if he has chosen you to mentor I think you should be grateful, not suspicious. Do you remember that quotation Bernie shared with you?"

"Yes, I've been thinking about that. 'Leadership should be born out of the understanding of the needs of those who would be affected by it'."

"Well, think about that, Mike, and think about what Bernie said about Russ, that he isn't capricious, never does anything random or arbitrary and always acts in the best interest of the company. This is the CEO of your company who is giving you strong indications that he thinks you have talent worth developing.

"If that isn't a valid answer to your question, Mike, you must just like asking the question. I'm sure with all that you have to think about you're not ready to go to sleep, but I am. I'll see you in the morning, and I'll be okay with whatever your answer is. But if you're still asking the question, I give up."

With that Alice gave me a kiss on the cheek and went upstairs to bed. She was right, I couldn't sleep at that point; I had to answer the question.

The Leadership Bridge

Leadership should be born out of the understanding of the needs of those who would be affected by it.
Marian Anderson

As a leader you will always be challenged with blending the wants of the organization and the wants of employees. Here is where the conflict lies; every organization has a fundamental desire to succeed and employees want to be successful in their work. Organizations use strategic plans, operational plans and human resources plans; however these planning tools hardly ever take into consideration the staff skills necessary to carry out the organizational plans.

Here is where you come in. You must become the bridge that spans the gap between the organization's goals and visions with your individual role of leading your section and department. You must effectively lead even if you don't have all the information needed to complete your tasks or if you don't fully understand the directives of your managers.

The leader is tasked with finding the best and safest route to manage the gap. The three personal characteristics required of you to successfully bridge the gap can be described in three words: Be, Know, Do. These words form the foundation of the U.S. Army's Officer Leadership Training Course. The lessons learned from this training program are easily applied to our business. Let's take a closer look at these skills.

BE:

This is the most difficult of all to master consistently. It means you are a person of good character. You will always do the right thing regardless of the consequences. Pursuit of the truth is the greater good, ahead of personal gain.

It also means your word is your bond. If you say you are going to do something you just do it.

Your subordinates are counting on you to be predictable in

any situation based on the belief that you will always do the right thing. Some might call it ethics others may call it a code of conduct. But whatever name you wish to use people expect you to operate with the highest standards.

KNOW:

You must have total command of your job knowledge, skills and applications and work continuously at improving those skills. Also seek out complementary skills to enhance effectiveness in your current position. Focus on commanding a working knowledge of the skills required for the position above and below yours.

The more you can relate to and communicate with all the skill levels of the people you work with the faster you will gain rapport and enjoy success. Never forget that your subordinates are looking to you for answers and direction. So be a student of your environment, apply what you've learned to the job and teach what you've learned to your subordinates.

DO:

To the best of your ability do your job every single day. You may have the beginning of the flu, but do the job to the best of your ability. You may have been up late with your newborn, but in the morning do the job to the best of your ability. No matter what environmental conditions you find yourself in each day, do the job to the best of your ability.

When you consistently practice these three personal qualities you are setting high standards and demonstrating to your subordinates that they should have equally high standards.

An additional benefit is that you will bridge the leadership gap successfully and better match the organization's needs with staff skills to meet company goals.

John A. DiCicco and Kenneth E. Strong, Jr.

Notes and Action Plan

Chapter Five

Communication Takes Effort

I awoke very early the next morning after just a few hours of sleep. It was still dark when I got up so I quietly got ready and left for work without waking Alice. I had made a decision and I didn't even want to talk to her about it until I had followed through with it.

I stopped at a diner to kill some time because I didn't want to get to the office too early. I ordered breakfast and read the morning paper. It felt good to have finally made the decision and actually be able to focus on something other than should I or shouldn't I for the first time in many days.

I spent most of the night reviewing all my conversations with Russ and Alice, and the one with Bernie, as though they were tape recordings playing in my head. I finally admitted to myself that I was afraid to go after something and not get it.

As Alice pointed out, if I didn't get the promotion I would still have a job, so what am I really afraid of? Being a loser? What if I didn't even try but could have had the job? Now that *would* make me a loser.

I think I was questioning Russ's motives just to give myself another excuse not to apply for the job. And I realized that I have no reason to suspect that Bernie has any ulterior motives for saying the things he did. He's probably just trying to help me.

I paid my check and headed for the office. I wanted to be there when the Human Resources Director came in.

I didn't even stop by my office, but went straight to Human Resources and applied for the job. For the first time in a long time I felt really good about myself. I got to my office just in time to hear a fax transmission coming through. It was unusual to get anything on the fax until an hour or so after the workday starts, so I picked up the message.

It was brief and to the point and from Russ. It said, "Meet me at our usual spot in the cafeteria at noontime. We have a lot to discuss! Also, I want you to think about this:"

Ask others about themselves, at the same time, be on guard not to talk too much about yourself.
                    Mortimer Jerome Adler

The morning seemed to drag by because I was so eager to meet with Russ and tell him that I had applied for the director's position. I wanted to get some guidance and advice from him about how to conduct myself at the interview. And that quotation about not talking too much about yourself made me think of something Alice said last night. When I was surprised that she knew so much about Bernie, and I knew so little, she said that people like to talk about themselves to someone who is interested.

I was so deep in thought that I was startled when the telephone rang. It was Human Resources, calling to schedule an interview with me at the end of the week. Well there's no backing out now. I'm definitely going to go for it.

I kept glancing at the clock all morning, willing it to be lunchtime. Finally a glance was rewarded and it was time to go to lunch and have a talk with Russ. While I was standing in line in the cafeteria Russ walked in with some people I'd never seen before. I wondered if they were the same people he had met with the week before.

I was really eager to tell Russ I already had an appointment for my first interview, but it didn't look as though he would be joining me any time soon. Judging by their expressions, the discussion he and his visitors were having was very serious.

Russ didn't even glance my way so I went to our usual meeting spot and sat down. I thought I'd just take my time with my lunch and maybe he'd join me before I was finished. I had nursed my coffee so long it was cold and I was just getting ready to leave when I saw him shaking hands with his visitors and then laughing with them heartily as people often do at the end of a meeting to break the tension. He walked them to the door, shook hands once more and headed directly to my table.

He asked what was good on the menu, I made a recommendation and he quickly got his lunch and returned to the table. He apologized for being late and said the people he was meeting with were representatives of a consulting company that Crown had hired to integrate some new technology that would be vital to the company's future.

I wasn't sure why he was telling me this, but I nodded to indicate that I understood. He looked at me as though he was expecting me to say something and when I didn't he said, " We only have a few minutes today. What have you got for me?"

"My first interview is scheduled for the end of this week!" I blurted out.

He just looked at me for a few seconds and then said, "And?"

"And what?" I replied.

"Nothing," he said, "I just thought you were going to add something to your statement."

"No, I just thought you might like to know."

"Know what?" he asked, adding, "Mike, I don't have time to waste and I don't like idle chatter."

I felt myself getting very angry, but tried to answer calmly, "I'm sorry, I didn't know that I was wasting your time."

Before I could say anything else he just looked at me with what I can only describe as a knowing expression and asked, "Did you get my fax this morning?"

I nodded to indicate that I had and he asked, "Did you read the message?" I nodded again and he added, "Think about it! I have to run now, but we'll talk tomorrow."

With that he stood up and quickly walked away, leaving me feeling somewhat deflated and wondering why he turned on me like that, and took no interest at all in what I told him. I thought he wanted me to apply for the supervisor's job and when I told him I had he said I was wasting his time! He seemed really annoyed with me and he's usually pretty calm.

I went back to my office and got to work, mostly to keep from thinking about Russ. When I stopped to have coffee later in the afternoon I picked up the fax and thought about what Russ had said and how he had acted.

We only had a few minutes to meet and he didn't even react to my news about my upcoming interview. He seemed to think that I should be responding to him. Then it hit me.

Ask others about themselves, at the same time, be on guard not to talk too much about yourself.

Russ confided in me about the consulting firm and my response was to talk about me. He volunteered important information about the company's future and I didn't ask any questions about his trip last week, or this meeting with the consulting company or what it would mean to the company's future. I just wanted to talk about my future. What a bonehead!

I suppose Alice was trying to make the same point Russ was when she talked about her conversation with Bernie and said that people like to talk about themselves when they have an interested listener. I'm getting the message that I would do well to listen more and talk less. And I'm going to have to try to keep that quotation in mind.

I think I'll ask Alice about that when I get home, but only after I tell her that I have an answer now to the big question.

Communication Takes Effort

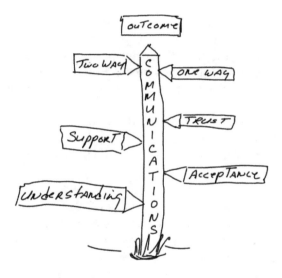

We must never forget that the most powerful communication isn't what you say; it's what you do. What counts, in the final analysis, is not what people are told but what they accept. It is this concept of the role of communication in industry that characterizes effective leadership.

Frank E. Fischer

The majority of people who are considered excellent conversationalists will tell you that they spend far more time listening than speaking. They also ask questions for clarification, making sure they fully understand what is being said before contributing their own thoughts about the topic.

This, as you may know, is easier said than done. It takes practice, practice and more practice.

Chances are when you are participating in a conversation you are listening from a defensive posture to interject your views at the expense of the other individual. Part of the reason for this is that we are emotionally bonded to our views. Believing in your views is a good thing except when the evidence suggests that they are not correct. Don't be so possessive of your views that you will not change them in a heartbeat when presented with contrary evidence.

The best way to ensure that you are listening completely is to imagine that you mind's inner voice is a tape recorder. As the person speaks repeat everything that is said in your mind's inner voice. This process helps you in a variety of ways.

You are not going to interrupt the conversation prematurely because you are repeating what is said in your mind and you are increasing your understanding of the issue because you first hear it then you repeat it.

The next step is to ask questions of clarification or check for understanding. Once the question is asked start the process all over again. Continue this process until the other person has finished their discussion. Once you fully understand the other person's position or point of view you can begin to present your view.

This process takes time, however the long- term benefits are that you will be considered a leader who is trustworthy, understanding, supportive and accepted by the people who you supervise and those who supervise you. You will immediately distinguish yourself as a leader worthy of being followed.

There will be times when it is not possible to have a two-way conversation, to gather ideas, suggestions and options. One-way communication should be reserved for emergencies, deadlines and directives after you have considered all the views, options and suggestions of your team to make the final decision.

The final outcome is to make far more good decisions than poor judgments. If things do go wrong, bring your team together to review how the poor outcome could have been avoided and prevent it from occurring next time. Some may call this process quality improvement and others call it an after action report. It doesn't matter what you call it; the process is what is important.

Your success as a leader depends on how good a listener you are and the quality of your questions. You may think that as a leader you should control the conversation. Perhaps you don't believe that can be done when you are repeating, in your mind, everything that is said and asking clarification questions. Think of it this way. When you ask an informed question based upon what you have heard and repeated, aren't you really determining the direction of the conversation?

Active listening, mentally repeating what is said and asking clarification questions, are a win/win process for everyone involved.

John A. DiCicco and Kenneth E. Strong, Jr.

Notes and Action Plan

Chapter Six

Pencil Down and Listen Up

After dinner the children went to their rooms to do their homework and Alice and I went to the family room. The television set was on but we weren't really watching it. We were each waiting for the other to break the silence.

After a few minutes I said, "Well, I have an answer for you."

"What," Alice said, in mock surprise, "No more questions?"

"Oh I have one of those too, but it's not a question that's going to exasperate you."

"Good, let's hear the answer."

"I applied for the director's job today and I have an interview scheduled for the end of the week."

"That's wonderful, Mike. And I just know you'll get the job."

"Of course I hope so, but if I don't it won't be the end of the world. I will still have a job."

"That sounds familiar. I think I heard someone else say something like that recently," Alice said with a smile.

"Yes you did, Honey, and my talks with you helped me think through to this decision."

"Anytime. It goes with the territory. Now what is the question?"

"I met with Russ in the cafeteria again today. I was so eager to tell him I had applied for the job that I behaved like a real bonehead."

"I think we all have a little bonehead in us. What did you do, slurp your soup in your eagerness to get through lunch?"

"I wish it had only been that. Russ was out at a meeting all day the day before, meeting with some representatives of an outside organization. The talk around the office was that it was something pretty big. While I was waiting for my lunch he came in with some of them.

"They stood around having what looked like a serious discussion until I was almost ready to go back to work. Then they left and Russ grabbed a quick lunch and joined me." I paused and shook my head as I thought back to the incident.

"If there's a point here, I'm missing it," Alice said, frowning slightly.

"Russ told me that the people he was meeting with were representatives of a consulting firm just hired to integrate some new technology that would mean a lot to the company's future. I sort of nodded to show that I understood and he just looked at me as though he was expecting me to say something.

"We only have a few minutes today, Mike," he finally said, "What have you got for me?"

I just blurted out that I had an interview for the supervisor's job scheduled for the end of the week.

Then he said, "And?"

And I said, "And what?"

And he said he just thought I was going to add something to my statement and I said something like, I thought he would like to know.

Then he said, "Know what?" And added that he didn't have time to waste and he didn't like idle chatter.

"That really made me mad, Alice, but I held my temper and just said, "I'm sorry I didn't know that I was wasting your time."

"Did he leave on that note?" Alice asked.

"No, he just looked at me as though he knew what I was thinking and asked me if I got the fax he sent me that morning. It was one of his quotations. I nodded and he asked if I had read the message and I nodded again.

"Then he said, "Think about it! I have to run now, but we'll talk tomorrow." And then he left.

Alice asked, "Do you remember the quotation?"

"I remember it and I'm going to try never to forget it.

'*Ask others about themselves, at the same time, be on guard not to talk too much about yourself.*'"

"And what was the question you had for me?"

"Do you remember that when you told me about your one and only conversation with Bernie, I asked how you could learn so much about him when I've worked with him for years and didn't know him at all?"

"Yes," Alice said, "I remember."

"When you said that it was because people like to talk about themselves to an interested listener, were you trying to tell me I don't listen enough and talk too much?"

"That wasn't my intention at the time, Mike, I was just giving you an honest explanation. But to be perfectly honest, you aren't the world's best listener. That quotation could have been written with you in mind."

"I'm afraid you're right, Alice, I don't think I can deny that. But Russ sent me that quotation early in the morning. How could he know then what I'd say at lunch?"

"Perhaps he knows more about you than you realize. Or maybe he was making the point that a good leader must be a good listener. He has sent you a number of quotations you could interpret to be directed to you as an individual, but maybe he is simply defining the qualities he considers essential in a leader. And I believe you are the guy who told me that leaders are made, not born."

"That's something I know for sure from my Army experience. I saw leaders made; I helped make some.

"And remember that Russ's last words to you were, we'll talk tomorrow."

"That's right and I'm not going to let this throw me, Alice. I've decided to go for that job and I'm not going to change my mind because of one incident."

"Now that sounds like a director talking," Alice said.

That was a happy thought to go to sleep on and I was feeling pretty good about things the next morning and looking forward to my meeting with Russ.

When I got to my office there was a fax waiting for me. It was another quotation:

You never will be the person you can be if pressure, tension and discipline are taken out of your life.
Dr. James G. Bilkey

Lying on my desk was a napkin with a sketch of a pencil and the words "pencil down and listen up."

I had a busy morning and by the time I got to the cafeteria Russ was at our usual spot, eating his lunch. I quickly got mine and joined him. He continued eating and gestured for me to do the same.

"How is your day going?" I asked.

"It's going well," he said, between bites, "That's a start."

I didn't know if that meant it was a good start on his day or if it meant that he realized that I was trying to take an interest in others and not just myself. But he said nothing more and just stared out the window as if I wasn't there.

I just kept eating my lunch and when I was finished Russ looked at me and said, "I'm here, I'm available to you and you're not talking to me."

This from the guy whose message yesterday was that I should listen more and talk less.

Then he said, "How do you propose to be a leader?"

I looked at him blankly. "I don't know what you mean."

"You read the fax, right?" he asked. When I nodded he added, "And you read the napkin with the drawing that said pencil down, right?"

I said, "Yes, and?"

"Well," he said, "What do you think it means?"

"I don't know," I said in frustration, "You're really confusing me."

"A leader doesn't have the luxury of being confused," he snapped, "You were in the military, you know that a confused leader can cost lives. In business it can cost jobs. But tell me why you are confused."

"I got the message about listening, and I've been doing that. Now you tell me I'm not talking to you. Are you just trying to put me under pressure, I asked?

"Maybe, and think about why I might do that. And when I talk about listening, Berber, I mean *really listening*. You have to think on your feet as well as do a lot of focused listening. You have to listen *and* process. You're confused because you don't think I always send a clear message. If you think I'm arbitrarily putting you under pressure, reread the quotation I sent you today.

"Listening helps to reduce a high percentage of confusion by allowing you time to take the focus off you and place it on the individual speaking to you. It lets people know that they are important to you."

I didn't say anything for a few seconds, and then said, "Yes, I see that."

"Good," Russ said, "And remember, there's a lot more to being a leader than intelligent listening. I have to go now, but I'll see you here at the usual time the day after tomorrow."

As he got up to leave, I tried to express my appreciation for how much he had helped me. He stopped me cold by patting me on the back and saying, "I'll see you here the day after tomorrow."

It was only three days until my interview and I was grateful that Russ would meet with me before then. I had finally made a conscious decision to be a leader and as difficult as it might be, I was determined to do it.

Pencil Down and Listen Up

Ask others about themselves, at the same time, be on guard not to talk too much about yourself.
Mortimer Jerome Adler

Being accessible makes you more valuable to the people you lead and the organization. Staff must feel comfortable approaching you when they need to. The benefits to you are that you keep your finger on the pulse of the organization and are better equipped to avert problems and take advantages of opportunities as they occur.

Also by using your accessibility as a teaching tool in the form of probing questions you are creating a training session that conditions your subordinates to think through their concerns, questions or problems. Your work time as a leader is just as valuable as your subordinate's. Don't waste it by being the answer man or woman.

There are always exceptions to the rule. You will be giving direction in emergency situations or when facing time deadlines.

More often than not people know the right answers and as leaders we have the obligation to create an environment that supports thinking out loud and the confidence to express views, questions, comments and concerns without fear or judgment.

You are a confidence builder, not a creator of self-doubt. Become a force multiplier. Teach your staff to think by effectively using questions rather than statements or directions.

Let's talk about listening. Most of us listen with the intent to respond immediately to views that do not conform to our own. In our desire to get our point across much of the information being given to us is lost because we are too busy formulating a response.

This attack listening causes some important interpersonal problems. First you are sending a negative message that says you do not value the information and the individual presenting it.

Second you are demonstrating a lack of respect for the individual and sending the message that only your views and opinions are important.

The result is that employees will not come to you and share information, comments, suggestions or concerns. As a result your performance and your company's will suffer. It may even lead to the loss of your job. The fastest way to become an ex-leader is to be known as someone who does not listen.

I am sure you have heard the reason God gave us two ears and one mouth is that we're supposed to listen twice as much as we speak.

The best way to ensure that you are listening twice as much as you speak is simply to shut up and listen.

Try the following techniques to improve your listening skills.

1. Repeat in your mind's voice every word that is being said to you. Think of it as echoing what you hear. I

guarantee you won't be blurting out responses. Practice this skill during your commute, repeating in your mind's voice what you hear on the radio. An added benefit of using this technique is you will remember information you hear more easily and more completely.

2. Ask questions for clarification using a thoughtful, gentle tone of voice.

3. Nod your head; use the standard non-verbal um hums.

4. Look the person in the eyes and ask if he or she would mind if you took a few notes. People are always flattered when you ask permission to take notes.

5. Prior to giving your response summarize what was said to you. Making this extra effort demonstrates that you listened intently and understood what was said. If no correction is necessary, make your response.

Studies have demonstrated that the best conversationalists are the best listeners, who ask specific questions that help to move the conversation along. When you take a step back and think about who controls the conversation, it's the person asking the questions.

So there is no need for you to practice attack listening. You will get your views across through the questions you ask and your staff will have tremendous trust and confidence in you. Everybody wins with good listening skills.

Silences make the real conversations between friends. Not the saying but the never needing to say is what counts.
                                        Margaret Lee Runbeck

John A. DiCicco and Kenneth E. Strong, Jr.

Notes and Action Plan

Chapter Seven

Balance Strength With Heart

The day before my interview, the day I was meeting with Russ at lunchtime, finally dawned.

That morning seemed like it lasted a week. When it was finally time for lunch I couldn't get to the cafeteria fast enough. Russ walked in at the same time I did and I interpreted that as a good sign.

Then I laughed inwardly at myself for attaching such significance to something so insignificant. I gave myself a silent warning to get a grip, exchanged pleasantries with Russ and we got our lunch and seated ourselves in a far corner of the cafeteria.

Neither of us spoke for several minutes, but for the first time I didn't find it an uncomfortable silence.

Russ finally said, "Are you apprehensive about the interview tomorrow?"

"I'm looking forward to it, but I do have some questions I'd like to ask you."

"Ask away, that's why we're here, Mike."

"Russ, we've talked a lot about intelligent listening and listening more than you talk, but in the interview wouldn't as much talking as possible make a better impression than just sitting there, silent, listening most of the time?"

"Mike, how much do you know about the position, the specific responsibilities, where it fits in with the organization, what kind of growth opportunities it offers?

"Not much, Russ, that's why I think it's important that I make a good impression."

"That doesn't make sense, Mike. How are you going to make a good impression by talking about something you know very little about, to people who know everything about it?"

"I see what you mean. I guess all I can do is answer their questions as honestly and completely as I can."

"That's a given, Mike. What is really key in this interview is that you listen and answer the questions carefully and intelligently, and ask your questions just as carefully and intelligently."

"I really want this job, Russ, and I want to make the most of this opportunity tomorrow."

"And I just told you how to do that. The purpose of this interview is not to learn how the company can meet your desires, but to see if you are a good fit for a leadership position and for this company and its growth."

"I know that, and I think I'm the right person for the position. I want to move up."

"A leadership role isn't a bed of roses, Mike. Not everyone is suited for it. The rank and the privileges come at a price. Leaders have to make decisions because they are right, not because they are popular.

"Good leaders often take the flack for mistakes made by their subordinates; that's one of the things that makes them good leaders. Wanting to be a leader because you want to move up doesn't make you a leader."

"Russ, you're starting to confuse me again. You encouraged me to apply for this position. You told me you thought I had it in me to be a leader."

"Yes, I did. And I do think that. But you need to understand that being a leader isn't all about you. It's about the people you lead and the company you lead them for. What's that expression from your Army days, about the men and women you lead?"

"You have to take care of your troops."

"And in business the people who work for you are your troops. If you're not there for them, they won't be there for you. And you can't be a leader no matter how much you want to get ahead, if no one will follow you. It can't be all about you."

I didn't say anything for a few seconds. I realized that Russ may just have kept me from having a disastrous interview, but I didn't know how to adequately express my appreciation.

Finally I found my voice and said, "Thank you, Russ. I appreciate what you've said here today more than I can express."

"And why is that, Mike?"

"Because you've made it crystal clear to me that if we hadn't had this talk I would have put my worst foot forward and given a negative and inaccurate impression of myself."

"I think you're right about that. I'm not going to wish you good luck tomorrow, because luck should have nothing to do with it. Just remember all the things we've talked about over the past weeks, and remember that you've been a leader."

With that Russ got up, gave me a thumbs up and left the cafeteria. I sat there for a few minutes, thinking over all our conversations and the napkin notes, and really understanding, for the first time, how much Russ had done for me over the past weeks. And I hadn't exactly been a quick study.

I knew I had a lot to learn, and I knew it wouldn't be easy, but I was determined to do it, starting with the interview tomorrow.

I finally managed to put the interview out of my mind and cleaned up my paperwork. I made a quick trip to the cafeteria for coffee just before quitting time and when I returned to my office there was a napkin lying on my desk. The quotation was a long one:

> *I wonder if the human touch, which people have, is not one of the greatest assets that one can have. You meet some people, and immediately you feel their warmth of mind or heart. You read a book, sit before the performance of a fine actor, or read a poem - and there it is – something that streams into your consciousness. Those who keep climbing higher, in their chosen work, all have this outstanding something. The nurse in the hospital, the man who delivers your mail, the clerk behind many a store counter, and the effective minister or public speaker. Without this human touch, hope has little on which to feed or thrive.*
>
> George Matthew Adams

Balance Strength With Heart

Let's face facts, in a leadership role you are paid for making hard decisions that others don't want to make and perhaps can't make. You may remember the old saying "rank has its privileges but also its responsibilities." It's only half right when you focus on the privilege of rank or status of your position.

To be an effective leader you must have a balanced approach between accomplishing the objectives of the organization and the needs of the individuals doing the work. It simply boils down to being as fair as possible to both sides. You can be a hard nosed leader; just be fair. People will work very hard for you if they don't like you or your style but they will go out of their way to destroy you if they hate you.

You may be called upon to make a decision that is contrary to what everyone else is doing.

Right is right even when no one else is doing it. Wrong is wrong even when everyone but you is doing it. Too often a leader is driven to satisfy his or her manager, stockholders, board of directors and his or her individual goals that may be contrary to what is the right thing to do.

All eyes are on you, whether you like it or not; as a leader you are constantly mentoring and setting the example. Everyone is watching to see what you are going to do. Always do what is right based upon your values, moral and ethical compass regardless of the consequences.

It takes personal courage and risk to your career to do the right thing.

These hard decisions are not made in a vacuum without impacting the lives of the people you work with and for. Always keep the welfare of the people you work with in mind when making your decisions.

John A. DiCicco and Kenneth E. Strong, Jr.

I wonder if the human touch, which people have, is not one of the greatest assets that one can have. You meet some people, and immediately you feel their warmth of mind or heart. You read a book, sit before the performance of a fine actor, or read a poem — and there it is — something that streams into your consciousness . . .. Those who keep climbing higher, in their chosen work, all have this outstanding something. The nurse in the hospital, the man who delivers your mail, the clerk behind many a store counter, and the effective minister or public speaker. Without this human touch, hope has little on which to feed or thrive.

George Matthew Adams

Chapter Eight

The Horizon Paradox

I felt surprisingly calm the morning of my interview. I took Alice's suggestion about which tie to wear and gave my shoes a great spit shine polish. Alice gave me the once over just before I left.

"Do I pass inspection, Alice?" I asked with a smile.

"Your suit is perfect, there's not a hair out of place, your shoes are blindingly shiny and the tie was an excellent choice. You look like a department director," she replied.

"Exactly what I had in mind," I said. "I read somewhere that you should dress for the job you want, not the job you have."

"Maybe by tonight you'll have the job you want instead of the job you have."

"Not likely. There are other candidates for the position and a number of people will be participating in the decision. The new director probably won't be named until shortly before Joe leaves."

"I thought Russ would make the decision."
"He has final approval, of course, but he doesn't make the decision alone."

"Okay, so it will take a little longer. That doesn't change the fact that you look like a director and I'm confident that you're going to be a director."

"Thank you for that supportive and highly objective opinion."

I said in a mock serious tone.

"You really feel good about this, don't you, Mike?"

"Yes I do, Alice. I know I'm not a shoo-in, but I do feel positive about it."

"It's so good to see you like this. You seem more like your old self than you have for years and years."

" I've done a lot of thinking in the past few weeks, Alice. It all started the night I went to the emergency room."

"That was a scary night."

"I know how scary it was for you and it was a real wake up call for me. When I admitted to myself that I was so afraid to make a decision that it resulted in what amounted to a panic attack, I took a real close look at myself and I didn't like what I saw.

"I was going to pass up an opportunity for a promotion because I was afraid I might not get it, or if I did get it that I'd have to take on new challenges.

"Instead of seeing Russ's mentoring as an opportunity, I looked for ulterior motives on his part. I've been selling myself short for a long time, and not even trying to achieve my potential. I've been afraid to have goals because I was afraid I might not achieve them. I'm not going to let my past direct my future any longer. The old me is back and he's here to stay."

"And it's great to have you back."

"And it's good to be back." Just keep your fingers crossed and think positive thoughts." Alice gave me a hug, opened the door and when I got to the car and looked back at the doorway she was waving goodbye with four pairs of crossed fingers.

I just had time to go to my office and check for messages

before the interview. There was a message from my boss, Joe Berringer, asking about my progress on the project and saying that he would like to see me in his office at two. I called his secretary, said I'd be there and went to the interview.

The interview lasted for an hour and a half.

Three senior staff members asked questions, questioned answers and generally x-rayed my mind. When I left the interview, I went straight to the cafeteria to get a good, stiff cup of coffee.

Just as I got back to my office Bernie, the Director of Financial Services, stuck his head in the door and said, "This must be interview day. You're looking like a serious contender."

"I just finished the interview. It was a pretty intense hour and a half."

"You seem to be bearing up," Bernie said, "It must have gone well."

"I feel pretty good about it, Bernie. It was challenging, but I enjoyed the challenge."

"That doesn't surprise me, Mike, you just needed to get your head in the right place," Bernie said, gave me the thumbs up sign and left.

You just needed to get your head in the right place. Those words kept running through my mind. Bernie's words were so simple, yet so profound. And he was right on target. That's exactly what has been wrong. I had my head in the wrong place. I have been hiding from who I really am, making excuses for being afraid to take risks, blaming others because I wasn't succeeding.

Keeping a low profile and opting for security wasn't the way to reach my goals, so I gave them up. I had become so afraid of failing that I wouldn't take any risk I could avoid.

I have great hopes of becoming the director of my department, but if I don't, there will be other opportunities and I'm going to be ready for them. I am not going to settle anymore. I have my head in the right place now and I'm keeping it there.

When I checked my messages I saw that Russ had left a message very early this morning asking me to meet him for coffee in the cafeteria at three. The unwelcome thought crossed my mind that I'd been demoted from lunch to coffee. But I told myself to stop that kind of thinking. Russ wants to meet with me and that is a positive thing. I'm not going to look for negative motives from a man who has done nothing but help me.

I spent the morning and early afternoon doing preliminary work on the big project and went to Joe's office promptly at two. Joe greeted me cordially and got right to the point of the meeting.

"Mike, I wanted to give you some background on this project you're working on. You don't have the full scope of the project yet, and we need to talk more about that, too. I told you that getting this customer is critical for Crown."

"I understand that, Joe, and I assure you that I'll do whatever has to be done to have it ready and have it right."

"I know you will, Mike, but you need to know that it isn't just critical for the company, it's also critical for you and for me."

"What do you mean, Joe, it's critical for you and me? What's critical for the company is critical for all of us, isn't it?"

"Yes, to some extent, but the success of this presentation will make or break this deal. And you and I are responsible for the presentation. I don't want to leave Crown on a sour note by losing the biggest business opportunity they have ever had. And with you in the running for my position you can't afford to be part of that loss."

"Agreed, but what is your point, Joe?"

"My point, Mike, is that I want to be certain that I make it crystal clear just how important this deal is and how much of our success depends on you. You're looking at an incredible number of hours of preparation. You will choose your own team and you'll have a lot of support, but you and I will be responsible for the results and I will be responsible for the presentation.

"I don't have the degree of technical expertise you have, so you'll have to get me up to speed on that. I am very comfortable making presentations, but I've never had to deal with anything as technically complex as this and I need to be able to explain it clearly to others whose technical knowledge is minimal."

"How many people will I have on my team?"

"As many as you need. Russ wants to talk to you about that, but you will make the choices."

"Okay. Now just what is the scope of this project?"

"It's a cutting-edge, integrated, computerized order and fulfillment distribution program for the largest international company in that sector."

"Are you talking about *Get It There?*"

"That's exactly what I'm talking about. This is so huge, Mike, it's hard to grasp its magnitude."

"We certainly have our work cut out for us. But what an opportunity! I'll talk to Russ and get back to you the day after tomorrow with a preliminary schedule."

"That's great, Mike. I'm really looking forward to working with you on this."

Joe walked me to the door, shook my hand, and looked as though I had taken the weight of the world off his shoulders. I hoped I could justify his faith by getting him up to speed technically in time for the presentation.

I didn't have long before my meeting with Russ, but I spent it productively, considering who I would like to have on my team. I had a pretty good idea who I wanted and who I didn't and I was starting to get psyched about the project. Now I understood why Joe was so concerned about the presentation.

I went to the cafeteria promptly at three, got some coffee and sat down just as Russ came in. He joined me and asked if I'd had my interview that morning. I said that I had.

"Well, how did it go?"

"It was an hour and a half of non-stop questions. There were their questions, my answers, my questions and their questions about my answers *and* myquestions.'

"How do you think you did, Mike?"

"I think I did pretty well. It was intense and challenging and I actually enjoyed it."

"Good for you. It sounds as though it went well. Did you talk with Joe today?"

"Yes, just a little while ago."

"How do you feel about this project, Mike?"

"After my talk with Joe this afternoon I have a much better understanding of how important it is to the company and the company's future."

"You're not answering my question. I asked you how you feel about this project."

" It's a big challenge, but Joe told me I would get to choose my own team and that has me rather psyched. I have already given the team some thought. I know the project will take a lot of extra hours, but it's a great opportunity and I'm excited to be involved."

"No concerns?"

"I have one concern. Joe is really counting on me to get him up to speed on the complexity of some of the technical aspects so he can make a persuasive and understandable presentation."

"Why is that a concern?"

"Given Joe's level of technical expertise, I'm not sure that's doable."

"Then find a way to make it doable."

"You know I'll try, Russ."

"Trying isn't good enough. You have to do it. Joe's counting on you and I'm counting on you. Now let's talk about the team. What are you looking for?"

"I want someone from each major department who has the appropriate skills and can work effectively as part of a team. They have to understand that the standard for the project is excellence and be willing to stay committed to the project until it's completed, no matter what that takes. My choices are going to be based on what each member of the team can contribute.

"Anything else?"

"This won't always mean people with the most seniority or highest rank in the company. That could result in some hurt feelings."

"Don't make any choices based on avoiding hurt feelings. If we don't get the very best people for the project, a great deal more will be hurt than feelings."

"I'm going to have my team choices and a preliminary schedule for Joe the day after tomorrow. Do you want to be at the meeting?"

"No, I'll be out of town, but send a copy to my office," Russ said. Then he stood up, handed me a napkin and left. I hadn't even noticed that as we talked he had been writing something on a napkin. It read:

> *When we are motivated by goals that have deep meaning, by dreams that need completion, by pure love that needs expressing, then we truly live life.*
>
> Greg Anderson

I smiled as I left the cafeteria, nodded to myself, put the napkin in my pocket and thought about my immediate goal, to choose the team that would get Crown its biggest deal ever.

The Horizon Paradox

> *When we are motivated by goals that have deep meaning, by dreams that need completion, by pure love that needs expressing, then we truly live life.*
>
> Greg Anderson

Leadership Is a Choice

A leader is goal oriented and somewhat futuristic in his or her planning. Reaching long- range goals can be a daunting and frustrating endeavor. Sometimes you may think that you will never reach your goal because the end seems so far away.

That's the trouble with goals, you reach certain milestones and then something changes and the goal is pushed out further along on the timeline, just over the horizon. Goals are like the horizon; once you get there you still have more distance to travel. The horizon keeps moving forward and the closer you get the more it seems the journey will never end. The result is a loss of focus and high level of frustration. The closer you get to the horizon the further it moves away from you. It becomes a never-ending chase.

One way to eliminate this effect is to schedule a periodic turn around or coming about as a sailor would say. Your perspective is completely changed; now you can immediately and clearly see how far you've come. Seeing where you've come from and all that you have achieved gives you a greater sense of accomplishment, satisfaction, focus and fun.

It is much less what we do than what we think, which fits us for the future.

Philip James Bailey

The horizon in the form of your personal or professional goals is by its nature future looking. The future is always just outside our reach. Make periodic turn around a habit and appreciate the distance you have traveled on your journey.

John A. DiCicco and Kenneth E. Strong, Jr.

Notes and Action Plan

Chapter Nine

A Leader's Area of Focus

When I left Russ after our talk about selecting my team, I felt very positive about the project. Despite the challenges I knew would be inherent in that selection, I had a very can do attitude. But the next day, as I sat in my office looking at the names of the people I had chosen for the team, the challenges my choices could create seemed to have grown.

I felt positive about my choices. I had put together the best possible team to get the information we needed for the presentation, but they had been chosen not on the basis of their rank or popularity in the company, but on their skills and abilities and what they could contribute to the project. I had carefully selected people I saw as team players, who would commit the time and effort required to produce the excellent results that were essential to our success.

Despite Russ's reassurances that I shouldn't name people to the team for the purpose of avoiding hurt feelings, I knew it wouldn't go over very well with some of the people in the company with more time on the job or in more senior positions, who were not chosen for the team. And that might not bode well for my future at Crown, even if I did get the promotion. You can't be a leader if no one will follow you.

After reviewing my choices several more times I still felt confident that I had assembled the best possible team for the job at hand. I printed a copy for Russ, dropped it off at his office and went to the cafeteria for lunch.

I joined a table where three of the people I had chosen to be members of my team were sitting. Of course they didn't know that yet. We all had a pleasant, congenial, non-work related conversation that covered a variety of topics. The way those I hoped would become team members interacted with everyone at the table reinforced my belief that they were sound choices.

I returned to my office in a more positive frame of mind and gave myself a mini-lecture about second guessing decisions that had been well thought out. I was confident that I had made the best choices possible with the information at hand and rehashing those choices was a needless waste of time. It simply brought progress to a standstill.

I cannot render myself ineffective by failing to make a decision for fear of making a mistake. Of course I'll make mistakes. The only way I can avoid making mistakes is to do nothing and I no longer consider that an option. I have to trust my own judgment if I expect others to trust me.

And I decided that I'm not going to make any decision based on how it might affect a promotion. I certainly hope I get the promotion, but I've been given a project of great significance to this company and all the people who are part of it. My focus is going to be on leading that team to success.

I put that thought into action and got to work writing my agenda for the first team meeting. Tomorrow I will see prospective team members privately, give each of them a thumbnail sketch of the project and ask him or her to serve on the team. Anyone who chooses not to be on the team will be able to express that choiceprivately.

At the first meeting everyone will get an individual assignment, the project's timeline and the proposed schedule of future meetings, with the understanding that the schedule could change, based on progress and/or problems. When a scheduled meeting is changed or an unscheduled meeting called, as much advance notice as possible will be given.

There will be a written agenda for every meeting and everyone is expected to be prompt; meetings will begin on time and end on time.

Everyone is expected to participate and no ideas or suggestions will be criticized. Each team member is to be prepared, at each meeting, to present his or her progress as scheduled. Anyone unable to do that is to see me prior to the meeting to explain and reschedule that progress report.

Just as I finished writing, my phone rang. I glanced at the clock and was surprised to see how late it was. Russ had returned from his trip early and stopped in the office to check his mail and messages. He called to say he wanted to see me before I left. I had barely hung up the phone when he appeared at my door with my team selection list in his hand.

"Hello, Mike. I got your list here and wanted to let you know it has my approval so you can move ahead."

"Thanks, Russ. I was just writing the agenda and the ground rules for my first meeting. How was your trip?"

"Very worthwhile. I even got back early and had good connections on my flights."

"That's always a plus. Would you like to see my agenda and the ground rules?"

"No, Mike, that's not necessary, this is your baby, but I would like to know how you're going to announce your selections to the team."

"I'm going to see each of them individually tomorrow. I'll give each person a brief explanation of the project and his or her individual assignment and ask each person if he or she will serve on the team. Then I'll follow up with an E-mail of the agenda and ground rules."

"Good approach. Anyone who doesn't choose to serve won't have to say so in front of the whole group. That's smart."

"Of course I hope everyone will want to be part of the team, but you never know what may be going on in someone's personal life that would make working extra hours out of the question. And I don't want any reluctant team members."

Russ nodded in agreement, and then said, "This is a big and complex project, Mike. Have you considered selecting an assistant team leader to share the work load?"

"No, Russ," I said, "I didn't consider that, but I will. In addition to sharing the work load an assistant team leader could provide backup."

"Do you have anyone in mind, Mike?"

"Not yet, but after meeting with the team I'm sure I will."

"Good. I won't keep you any longer, Mike." "Just one other thing, Russ. About Joe."

"I hope you aren't having a problem with Joe."

"Oh, no. I know Joe doesn't want to be in on the planning and work sessions on this project, but I though I should invite him to the initial meeting to give him the recognition with the team that he is the man who is responsible for making the presentation."

"Good thinking. You know, Mike, I think you're getting smarter all the time."

"Well there's certainly room for growth in that area."

"That goes for all of us, Mike, that goes for all of us. See you tomorrow. Oh and here's a little something for you," Russ said, handing me a napkin as he walked out the door.

I unfolded the napkin and read the following quotation:

In the end, we do battle only with ourselves. Once we understand this and focus our energy on what we can do to control our lives....we begin to gain important insights into how life works.

H. Stanley Judd

I read the quotation and wondered, not for the first time, if Russ could possibly be reading my mind.

A Leader's Area of Focus

In the end, we do battle only with ourselves. Once we understand this and focus our energy on what we can do to control our lives....we begin to gain important insights into how life works.

H. Stanley Judd

One of the key areas on which the leader must focus is the nurturing and development of future and current leaders. Your focus must be on the areas that are by their very nature difficult and uncertain. You must be comfortable and confident with your own company because others will shy away from you if they think your assignment may fail.

Sometimes you will be a majority of one. Even when all around you doubt you and think you're crazy for taking such a big risk, take it anyway. As a leader, you must go into the areas where there is the greatest risk of failure or the greatest need for success. Embrace your fears and move forward. Lead from the front and others will follow.

As a point to begin a discussion these are my thoughts on leadership, which can best be described using an acronym, VOTE.

Vision: Seeing the big picture, knowing where you are going, why you are going there, and how you'll get there, is essential. Reasons come first; answers come second. Let nothing that doesn't violate a law or your character keep you from your goal.

Optimism: Having a sense that everything will work out and exhibiting that to staff is essential. Looking for the good and doable in every situation is reassuring to staff. All eyes are on the leader when things are difficult. You are both guide and cheerleader.

Trust: It is difficult at best to earn the trust of staff and once lost it can never be regained. Without the trust of your staff you have nothing and are ineffectual as a leader. Trust is an all or nothing proposition. People must know what you stand for. Trust must be earned.

Expedite: Doing things when they need to be done is important, regardless of their pleasantness or unpleasantness. You must act quickly and not wait for all the data to come in. Go with seventy percent of the information needed.

In many ways the leader of the future will be akin to the ancient Samurai, skilled with weapons, music, painting, poetry and a master at reading the environment that surrounds him or her. Miyamoto Musashi, in his classic guide to strategy, "The Five Rings," offers the following guidelines for leadership. *My interpretations of his guidelines are italicized.*

1. Do not think dishonestly
(Always be of good character)

2. The Way
(To success is in training)

3. Become acquainted with every art
(Organizational and political skills)

4. Know the Ways of all professionals
*(Working knowledge of all departments
in your organization)*

5. Distinguish between gain and loss in worldly matters
(Collect and evaluate data)

6. Develop intuitive judgment and understanding
for everything
(Trust your gut feeling)

7. Perceive those things that cannot be seen
(Trust your senses)

8. Pay attention even to trifles
(Small details)

9. Do nothing, which is of no use
(Stay focused on the desired outcome)

Cross training is critical to your success. If you are a generalist find a specialty, if you are a specialist become more of a generalist. Everything you have learned in life you will draw upon as a leader.

John A. DiCicco and Kenneth E. Strong, Jr.

Notes and Action Plan

Chapter Ten

Read The Book

The meetings I had with each of my team members went even better than I had hoped. Despite the minimum of details and the maximum of assurance that the project would be exacting and consume many extra hours, not one of them declined to serve. In fact, in varying ways, they all said that they considered it an honor to be asked to be part of a project that was so important to the company's future.

Their loyalty to the company and the obvious respect they had for Russ was impressive. When I was still questioning why Russ was taking an interest in me, encouraging me to apply for a promotion I wasn't even sure I wanted, Alice had an explanation for Russ's interest. She said she was sure I wasn't the first Crown employee Russ had taken an interest in because he saw qualities he wanted to nurture for the benefit of the company.

Given the positive reaction of all my team members to an opportunity to make a significant contribution to the company's future, I realized Alice had been right. And I also realized that I had the opportunity to lead a first class team to make that contribution. I glanced at the clock and realized it was time to head to our first team meeting. And I was eager to get started.

Just as I gathered up my materials for the meeting, Joe Berringer appeared at my door, looking very uncomfortable.

"Hi, Mike," he said, in an overly hearty tone. "Do you have a minute before you head off to your meeting? I need talk to you."

"Since we're heading off to the same meeting, Joe, let's talk on the way. And you can give me a hand with some of this stuff."

"Well you see, Mike, that's just the thing. I'm not going to the meeting."

"What do you mean, you're not going? We talked about this before I recruited my team, Joe. You said you didn't have a conflict and you would be there."

"Yes, I know, Mike, but I've been thinking about it and I don't think it's a good idea."

"Why not? You are responsible for making the presentation. You need to meet and express appreciation to this team for the hard work they are about to do on your behalf."

"Not on my behalf, Mike, on Crown's behalf."

"But we're all part of Crown, aren't we Joe?"

"Come on, Mike, I'm a lame duck. Everyone knows I've resigned. By the time this new client is on board you'll probably have my job."

"Maybe and maybe not, Joe. But in any event, that's then, and this is now. And right now you are the Director of the Department and you still work for Crown and you're the man who is going to make the presentation. You can at least come to the meeting and let the team know that you appreciate what they are doing."

"I can't answer any of their questions, Mike, and I don't want to stand up there and look like a fool."

"Joe, no one is going to ask you any questions. And I promise you that nothing will be said or done that will embarrass you. I need you to be there to show the team how important this project is and how much we need them and the work they are about to do. You owe that to Crown."

"You guarantee me there will be no questions I can't answer?"

"You have my word, Joe. All I expect of you is that you stay for the entire meeting, look interested and impressed and thank everyone, individually, at the end of the meeting for the task they are undertaking."

"That's all?"

"Absolutely. Now let's get going. I don't want to be late for my own meeting, and bring those papers there, will you?" I asked and walked out the door, without waiting for his answer, not even sure he was following me until someone passed us in the hallway and called Joe by name.

When I got to the meeting room, exactly on time, everyone was there. I introduced Joe, who everyone knew by sight, and talked him up as our flag bearer in the upcoming battle for company growth. Joe clasped his hands together and raised them over his head in the manner of a victorious athlete and won a round of applause.

There were two long tables set up in the front of the room and Joe and I had all but covered them with the materials we brought with us. There were manuals, specifications, budgets, proposed contracts, drawings, and innumerable documents with which I was not yet familiar.

After handing out the proposed schedule for future meetings and the scheduled completion date for the finished proposal, I gave the team time to take a cursory look at all the materials on the tables, knowing I would get innumerable questions I couldn't answer at this point.

Joe was looking very ill at ease and I realized he was anticipating questions he couldn't answer. I quietly told him that questions would be directed to me and assured him that he would not be asked any questions.

The team was engrossed in looking at the collection of

documents on the tables and taking the greatest interest in those relating to their specific area of expertise. When I saw the first signs of circuit overload I called them back to their seats.

"I'm pretty sure you all have a lot of questions. And you are free to ask them. But I'll tell you in advance that I don't have a lot of answers. A lot of this material is as new to me as it is to you. But let's hear those questions anyway, and please state your name and your department so we all get to know one another by name."

A young woman in the front row raised her hand eagerly, saying, "I'm Audrey Marshall and I'm in Human Resources. Much of the material displayed here today is completely out of my area of expertise. Is someone going to help me become familiar with it?"

"Absolutely, Audrey," I said. "You are. I expect each of you to assimilate as much as possible in all areas and everything in your particular area of expertise."

"I don't know how to read specifications and I've never read a budget," Audrey said.

"You will have when we're finished, Audrey," I said with a smile.

Then I addressed my remarks to the entire group, saying, "We're going to do a lot of cross training in the days ahead because a general understanding of the entire project is essential for everyone on the team. Take a risk, learn along the way, read all the materials, and return to the next meeting with questions based on your reading.

"I really don't understand how to read drawings, either," Audrey persisted.

"Audrey, no one is born knowing these things. They learn. And you'll learn," I said.

"But how?" she asked. "R.T.B., Audrey. R.T.B."

"I don't know what that means," she said.

"Read the book, or the contract, or the specifications. There are copies here for each of you. We will all learn as we go, both from the materials and from one another. I expect a lot of questions, but I expect informed questions.

"Ask questions after you have read the material. There will be no spoon-feeding here. I said that these meetings will begin and end on time, and it's almost ending time. But before we wrap it up I think Joe wants to say something."

Joe walked to the front of the room and said, putting every ounce of his charisma into it, "If I can do half as good a job with my presentation as I know this team is going to do in putting it together, this will be the most successful project Crown has ever undertaken. Thank you, to each one of you for the tremendous job I know you are going to do. On your way out of this meeting, I'd like to shake your hand and thank each of you personally."

This won him another round of applause as he gave his winning athlete victory wave and walked to the doorway through which everyone would leave. With that I adjourned the meeting.

As I gathered up the remaining materials on the tables, Audrey approached me and said, "I don't want you to think I am reluctant to take on a challenge. I am really eager to learn everything I can about all areas of the company."

"Even though you asked the questions, Audrey, I think they were on everyone's mind, and I'm glad you asked them."

She looked relieved at my answer and added, "I'm looking forward to this project and I'm glad to be part of it." Taking her armload of materials as she left the room she said, "Thank you for including me."

I caught up with Joe in the hallway, thanked him for his remarks and told him how well he had gone over with the team. "Piece of cake, Mike, anytime," he said, exuding confidence.

I hoped Joe's off again on again behavior wasn't going to be typical. But I put him out of my mind for the present and thought about what I considered a promising beginning of our Operation Challenge.

I went to lunch early, hoping to run into Joe and try to keep him pumped up about the presentation. He still hadn't come in by the time I finished, so I headed back to my office. I met Russ just outside the cafeteria and he asked how the meeting had gone. I told him it had gone very well and I was very impressed with my team.

"How did Joe do?" Russ asked.

"Just fine. He was vintage Joe, but I'm going to have to keep bolstering him up."

"Did your team seem apprehensive about the scope of the project?"

"I think they understand that it's quite a challenge, but they seem eager to begin. A young woman from HR, Audrey Marshall, asked a number of questions about some of the documents I took to the meeting, since she wasn't familiar with them and wanted to be assured that someone would teach her.

"I think she may have been expressing a concern many on the team shared. I assured them all that what they didn't know they would soon learn."

"And do you still think Audrey was a good choice for the team?"

"Absolutely. I was very impressed by what I read in her personnel file and I'm considering her for assistant team leader."

Russ smiled and said, "I think you may be ahead of me on this one, Mike," and handed me a napkin as he walked past me and into the cafeteria.

Of course there was a quotation. This one was from Abigail Smith Adams, " Learning is not attained by chance. It must be sought for with ardor and attended to with diligence."

As I read it I thought to myself that I certainly wasn't ahead of Russ, but I was beginning to get on his wavelength.

Read The Book

RTB

Read The Book

Learning is not attained by chance. It must be sought for with ardor and attended to with diligence.
Abigail Smith Adams

One of the most memorable lessons I learned in the Army was from Sergeant First Class Nolan. As a young Second Lieutenant in the Army Medical Corps, fresh out of the Academy of Health Sciences, I would often ask him, "What is the regulation on this or that?"

Apparently I asked him one time too many.

He put his pencil down, looked over his black rimmed military issue glasses, drew in a long breath and in a deep firm military voice said, "Lieutenant, R-T-B," and tossed me a five inch thick D ring notebook of regulations. I got the message.

There are no mistakes. The events we bring upon ourselves, no matter how unpleasant, are necessary in order to learn what we need to learn; whatever steps we take, they are necessary to reach the places we've chosen to go.
Richard David Bach

The lesson was clear. There are some things best to learn for yourself. You should never allow yourself to be at an informational disadvantage to the subject matter experts. We are moving into an area of generalization rather than specialization.

Many organizations are cross training employees to maintain organizational effectiveness or reduce the impact of a coming labor shortage.

You will be far more valuable to an organization as a generalist with a specialty than you will be as a specialist, especially as companies go through downsizing and other cost saving measures.

Chapter Eleven

The Sign On The Door Says So

The next day I had an E-mail message from Audrey asking if she could have a few minutes of my time before the end of the day. I responded that I would see her in my office around four.

I wondered if she was feeling overwhelmed by the project now that she had a better idea of its magnitude. But her comments to me at the end of the meeting certainly didn't bear that out.

If she wasn't up to the challenge it was better to find that out now, but I hated to lose a team member before we even got started. And I even had her in mind for my assistant team leader.

When I reviewed her personnel file all the indications were that she was bright, ambitious, hard working and always eager to take on extra assignments. Was my judgment of her completely inaccurate?

Then I caught myself. I was second-guessing my assessment of Audrey when I really had no idea why she wanted to see me. There was no reason to leap to the conclusion that her reason was negative. In any event, I'd know soon enough what she wanted and whatever it was, I'd handle it.

As I left the cafeteria after lunch Joe Berringer fell in step with me. We exchanged brief pleasantries and he said he had to stop by my office and tell me something important. Joe hasn't ever been the kind of boss who spends a lot of time with you, and since the announcement of his resignation I have seen even less of him.

I said, " Sure, Joe, come in and have a seat. What's up?"

"I hate to have to tell you this, Mike, but there's a lot of grumbling going on about the project."

"Who's doing this grumbling, Joe, the team?"

"No, I haven't heard anything like that. It's coming from people who weren't selected for the team, who have more senior positions and more history with the company than some of your team."

"I think that was probably to be expected." "But Mike, if they are resentful, they may not be cooperative with your people and you might not get all the information you need, or," and he grimaced, "the correct information."

"Are you putting me on, Joe, or are you actually suggesting that they would intentionally sabotage the project?"

Joe looked genuinely worried and said, "No, Mike, I'm serious. It's as important to me as it is to you that we get this contract. Remember I have to make the presentation and I don't want to be remembered as the guy who lost Crown the biggest contract in its history."

"That's not going to happen. I chose the people in the company with the best qualifications for this project and I'm not going to second guess my choices because some egos have been bruised. Russ assigned me to this project because he thought I could do it. And I can, and I will. Russ warned me there would be hurt feelings but he pointed out the loss of this contract would hurt more than the feelings of everyone in thecompany."

"Mike, I just thought you should know."

"I appreciate you telling me, Joe. Was there anything else?"

"Well, some of them were questioning why you are doing this when some of them have been here so much longer."

"Because I am the team leader and I am the team leader

because Russ said so. And Russ doesn't have to explain his decisions to anyone."

"I'm glad we had this talk, Mike. Your confidence must be contagious, I think I'm catching it."

After Joe left, I thought about Russ's supportive comments about my method of team selection and realized that had helped me keep Joe's well-intentioned warnings in perspective. I appreciated Joe's comment about my confidence being contagious. I did feel confident and I certainly wanted it to be contagious.

Audrey arrived promptly at four, closed the door at my request and took the chair I indicated. She seemed a bit nervous and reluctant to begin the conversation, so I decided to get right to it.

"What is it you want to talk to me about, Audrey?" I asked as soon as she was seated.

"I want to apologize to you."

"Apologize," I said, in a questioning tone. "For what?"

"For speaking out as I did at our initial meeting, questioning you as I did in front of everyone."

"And why do you think that requires an apology?"

"Well, I thought later that it might make others think I was questioning your knowledge, or your authority because you didn't have the answers."

"And you think the leader always has the answers?

"Not always, but usually."

"It's the leader's job to select the best answer, with the help of those he is leading, and to take the responsibility for it, but no one has all the answers, Audrey."

"After I thought about it, I was concerned that you would think I was challenging you and I wasn't. I think the scope of the project overwhelmed me at first. There were so many aspects of it that were new to me that the questions just came rolling out. I was so excited to be part of the team and I didn't want to let the team down."

"Audrey, you say that you were overwhelmed. Does that mean you aren't any longer?"

"Well I've had a chance to talk with other members of the team and I realize now that we all have different areas of expertise so we all have a lot of new things to learn. I'm certainly not diminishing the scope of the project. I realize it will be time consuming and often difficult, but I am confident that I can make a significant contribution."

"I was confident of that when I asked you to join the team. And there is nothing wrong with asking questions as long as they aren't being used as an excuse to learn for yourself."

"Thank you for understanding, Mike, I just didn't want to get off on the wrong foot."

"You didn't, Audrey. And I'm glad you came to see me. There's something I wanted to talk to you about. I'm going to need an assistant team leader and I'd like it to be you. Would you accept that role?"

"I certainly would."

"I want you to understand that it would mean even more extra hours than most of the team will be putting in."
"That's not a problem for me. I accept."

"Thank you. You're taking on a big job, and I appreciate it."

"And I give you my word that I won't disappoint you," she said, as she stood up, shook my hand and left the office.

As I left the office that evening I almost ran into Russ as he started in my door.

"I hoped you hadn't left yet, Mike. Can we talk for a minute?"

"Sure," I said, "Come in and sit down." "Just for a couple minutes, Mike. I saw Joe after he talked with you today. He told me why he came to see you and that you reassured him that you don't consider the grumblers a problem."

"Russ, when we discussed the team selection you assured me you supported my approach and pointed out that the company's future greatly outweighs a few hurt feelings or bruised egos. I have a good team and I'm not going to fix what isn't broken."

"Glad to hear it. Do you have an assistant team leader yet?"

"Yes. I asked Audrey today. She accepted with enthusiasm. I think she's going to be very good."

"It sounds like you had a pretty good day, Mike."

"Yes, I did. Of course some days are better than others, but every day I like this job a little bit more."

"You know, Mike," Russ said with a grin, "I'm beginning to believe you have actually been listening to me." With that he stood up, handed me a napkin he had folded in his hand and as he left the office I unfolded the napkin and read,

"The most dangerous leadership myth is that leaders are born—that there is a genetic factor to leadership. This myth asserts that people simply either have certain charismatic qualities or not. That's nonsense; in fact, the opposite is true. Leaders are made rather than born."
                                        Warren G. Bennis

John A. DiCicco and Kenneth E. Strong, Jr.

The Sign On The Door Says So

Very often leaders, especially newly appointed leaders, want so desperately to make an impact on their organization that they over control their subordinates. Some leaders try to demonstrate how much they know beyond what the supervisor knows about performing the job.

Such efforts to establish and justify their role as leader can cause an unnecessary morale problem and a lack of confidence in leadership. The result is the opposite of what was intended. Morale diminishes, the leader is criticized, perhaps even sabotaged; there is a breakdown in production and required outcomes are not met.

You must not focus on the day-to-day decisions but on the big picture; will you have the necessary resources, personnel, money or materials to conduct business.

As a leader you have nothing to prove because the sign on the door says you're the leader. Everyone knows you are the leader, manager or supervisor. Your manager will give you credit or blame appropriately without your proving to your subordinates that you are in charge.

Chapter Twelve

Spider Web Management

The team was making good progress in assembling the wealth of information needed to put the presentation together, but the bruised egos and hurt feelings were making themselves known. Team members who were chosen rather than one of their superiors were prime targets in their departments. And the team in general was hearing a lot of sniping and criticism, thinly disguised as humor, from their peers.

I knew that initially those who expected to be selected for the team based on their length of service or rank in the company would be critical, but I didn't expect it to last. Getting this contract was critical to the company's growth and would ultimately benefit every person who worked at Crown.

Even though Russ had communicated that, very clearly, before the team was chosen, the criticism, sniping and predictions of failure were beginning to affect the team. It was undermining their confidence and beginning to make them less supportive of one another. I asked Audrey to meet with me to schedule a meeting with all the team members. I glanced up at the clock and saw Audrey standing in my doorway.

"Audrey, come in and have a seat. Have you been standing there long?"

"No, just a few seconds. You were so deep in thought I didn't want to interrupt."

"I was just thinking about this meeting. Have you been getting any flak in your department?"

"A little. Comments are made so I'll be sure to overhear them."

"Such as?"

"Wouldn't you think they would want the people who have been here the longest on the team?"

"Have you ever responded to any of it, Audrey?"

"Only once, Mike. Someone said in a stage whisper they intended for me to hear, "Why on earth did they put her on the team instead of her manager?'

"In a stage whisper that was equally audible, I said, " Whoever is wondering should ask Russ Jacobs."

"I don't think anyone is going to be foolish enough to do that, Audrey."

"I'm sure of that, Mike, but why doesn't Russ address this issue?"

"Because that's my job, Audrey, not his. That's why we're going to have this meeting. We have to handle this ourselves. I can't call off the dogs. For that matter, neither can Russ. It's far easier to criticize and predict failure than it is to support and be optimistic. But the team can't let this negativity affect their work, this project is too important."

"How can you keep it from affecting the team?"

"By reminding them what a team is, how it functions and what is at stake."

"In other words, an old fashioned pep talk."

"Something like that. Now what is the soonest we can get everyone together?"

"We can have the largest conference room day after tomorrow and no one on the team will be out of town that day."

"Great. Reserve the room and here's the notice I want sent to everyone on the team by the end of the day."

"I see it's to be a lunch meeting. Would you like me to make the lunch arrangements?"

"Yes, thank you, I'd appreciate that, Audrey."

"Anything else I can do?"

"No, that covers it. I really appreciate your help."

"Good, then I'll get to it." And with that she left the office.

The next day and a half the office was buzzing with speculation about the purpose of the team lunch meeting. Those on the team were concerned that there were going to be some changes. Those who wished they were on the team were predicting that it was going to be disbanded and reformed to their liking.

When I entered the meeting room five minutes early, everyone was there and seated. I spoke to people as I made my way to the front of the room and as I turned the microphone on the room became quiet.

"I have a few quotations for you. I can't attribute them to any specific individual, but I have reason to believe many of you could. I'm not going to ask you to do that, because who said what isn't important. But when I finish I'm going to ask you to do something for me.

"I've been here for X (you fill in the blank) number of years. Why wasn't I asked to be on the team?"

"I'm not on the team, but someone I supervise is. How much sense does that make?"

95

"Their selection process must have consisted of pulling names out of a hat."

"With Berber's team working on it we can kiss that big contract goodbye."

"If any of these quotations are familiar to you, I'd like you to raise your hand. Don't hold back; if you've heard any of these or similar comments, just raise your hand."

Hands were raised slowly until everyone in the room had his or her hand up. One young woman from information technology raised both hands.

"Janice, I have to ask. Why do you have both hands raised?"

"Because I've heard all of them," she said, then added, "My office is very close to the water cooler."

That got a laugh of appreciation and a smattering of applause.

"I've heard many of them, second hand. I know that hearing negative, critical, demeaning comments can affect the way you view yourself, your fellow teammates and the project. And we just can't let that happen.

"Securing this contract will give Crown such growth that it will enable us to acquire new assets, purchase new equipment, improve benefits, increase salaries and become premier in our field. Failure to secure this contract is not an option.

"Criticizing and belittling is far easier than promoting and encouraging. Many of the people criticizing this team are angry at not being included on the team. Their feelings and their egos are hurt, so they go out of their way to find fault.

"There will be criticism of the team selection process, of our approach, our personalities, our lack of experience, but I guarantee you there will be no criticism when we secure the contract.

"We can't stop the criticism. But we can keep it from affecting our performance. We have to refocus on the job we were selected to do. Selected is the operative word here. Not entitled, not tenured, selected.

"We cannot let the critics of our team turn us into critics of one another. Finding fault can force people to fail and we cannot fail. We have to stick together, support one another and believe in one another, in our determination and our ability. We have to be a team in fact, not just in terminology.

"Each of you is on this team because I believe in you and the CEO of Crown believes in you. And you have to believe in yourself and in one another. I want to thank you for all the hard work you have done, for all the hard work you are going to do, and for staying focused on what is really important. Remember, we are going to secure this contract!"

My pep talk, as Audrey called it, got applause almost as enthusiastic as my announcement that lunch awaited us in the next room. As I headed toward the lunch area Russ appeared from the rear of the room. And of course he had a small paper napkin crunched in his hand.

"Hello, Russ, I didn't realize you were here. Why don't you join us for lunch?

"No thanks, Mike. You're their leader. You don't need me here. I've gotten wind of some of the grumbling and wanted to hear what you had to say. You handled that very well. And here's something for you."

"Thanks, Russ," I said as he handed me the inevitable napkin and headed for his office. I smoothed it out and as I read it I thought once again that Russ might well be a mind reader."

"I can live for two months on a good compliment."
Mark Twain

Spider Web Management

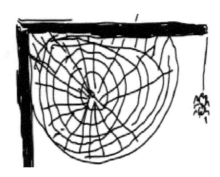

Much of our management training and practices is designed to find fault and assign responsibility. We design systems to evaluate deviations from norms and measure the impact of the variations. This effort on the part of managers is an attempt to improve things generating more efficiency and cost savings.

As a result of this long standing practice we have become good at discovering what is wrong with just about everything. Fact finding the negative results in work performance and what's wrong with life has become easy for us, too easy.

Perhaps it became part of our life experience when we started school. Think about when the business environment, its culture, political structure and a labyrinth of rules, regulations, workflows, systems and policies and procedures.

Yes, discipline and accountability are important and should not be minimized, but these business elements do not have to be punitive based. In the long run, by changing your focus to reinforcing positive behavior rather than focusing on negative enforcement, the organization will be far more successful.

Catch people doing things right!

I can live for two months on a good compliment.
Mark Twain

Chapter Thirteen

We Can Fix This

It was Monday morning and I was at my desk an hour and a half before the normal beginning of the workday. That wasn't unusual while we were preparing the big presentation for what, if we were successful, would become Crown's most important client ever.

Everyone on the team got to work earlier and stayed later than the other employees, but no one complained. I tried to be at my desk before anyone else on the team arrived, but frequently found someone on the job before me.

The long hours we were all putting in were being noted and the commitment the team was demonstrating had earned the respect of the rest of the employees, even those who had been the most critical. Perhaps they had finally realized that while the team was doing all the work, every person in the company would reap the benefits if we were successful.

I looked forward to going to work every day and took satisfaction in being part of what the team was accomplishing. We were getting close to the deadline for having the presentation ready and we were right on schedule. I had asked Audrey to come to my office to set up our presentation rehearsal schedule with Joe and the team. I looked up when I heard a light knock on my door, expecting to see Audrey. But it was Russ who hesitantly opened the door and asked, "Got a minute, Mike?"

Russ was probably a very good poker player. His expressions never gave anything away. He could have come to announce that the entire building was on fire, or that Crown's stock had just doubled in value and his expression would have been just the same. There was no point in trying to anticipate why he wanted to see me, so I simply got right to it.

"Sure, Russ. Have a seat. Do we have a problem?"

"Let's think of it as more of a challenge, Mike," he said, as he casually sat down.

"Can you make that more specific?"

"Joe isn't going to make the presentation."

"That's not even a challenge, Russ. Joe just needs another pep talk to bolster his confidence. Audrey and I are meeting in a few minutes to go over the schedule for preparing him on each phase of the presentation. He's just having a case of cold feet about the technical information. When I go over it with him and he sees how well prepared we are, he'll be fine."

"No, Mike, he's in the hospital in intensive care. He's had a serious heart attack."

"Oh, no! Is he going pull through?"

"It's too soon to tell, but everything possible is being done for him. At best I'm afraid he's in for a very long stay in the hospital."

" I think that's more of a problem than a challenge, Russ."

"Joe is the one with a problem, but that is out of our control, Mike. What we have is a challenge, not a problem, and we can do something about that."

"I get your point, Russ."

"You have been telling me that your team is doing a great job putting the presentation information together."

"Yes, and they are. But we were counting on Joe to make the actual presentation."

"Mike, I've heard you use an expression from your Army days, 'Improvise, adapt and overcome.' That's what's called for now, so I suggest you meet this challenge by doing just that. I'm confident that you will come through for us. This is an opportunity for your team, and you, to make a great contribution to this company's success. I'm counting on you and your team," he said as he left.

Russ was barely out the door when Audrey put her head around the corner of the doorway and said, "I'm a little early, would you like me to come back later?"

"No, Audrey, early is good today. Early is very good today. It seems that we have a new challenge."

"I passed Russ in the hall as he was leaving your office. Is something wrong? "

I explained to Audrey that Joe was in the hospital and wouldn't be able to make the presentation and it was up to the team to do it. After we exchanged our concerns for Joe we sat in the office in silence for a long time. Our minds were in overdrive, but neither of us spoke. Finally I suggested that Audrey go back to her office and return after lunch with her ideas.

"We can't spend too much time deciding what we're going to do, Audrey. We have to stay on schedule. Come back at two and we'll discuss our ideas and agree by the end of the day how we're going to proceed."

"Mike, I'll go along with whatever you want to do," she said.

"No, we'll lay out our ideas, discuss them, and put together the approach we agree is best. Then we'll present it to the team for their input. You and I have different perspectives, as do all the team members, and we have to come up with an approach everyone on the team supports. You are an important member of the team, Audrey and I value your input, not just your agreement."

"Thank you, Mike. I'll give it my best effort." "I know you will. I'll see you back here at two."

I returned to my office after lunch, if you can call four cups of coffee lunch, with a legal pad covered with more coffee stains than writing. But I was satisfied with what I had written and felt confident that Audrey's efforts would mesh with mine. I also had confidence that the team would further improve the plan.

At four o'clock all team members were contacted to come to a meeting at four-thirty. My confidence was not misplaced. After many expressions of concern for Joe, the team decided one member should be the team representative to maintain contact with Joe's wife and visit Joe when that was appropriate.

I outlined the tentative plan Audrey and I had developed. I would present the technical information and Audrey would cover all personnel issues. We needed to choose someone to cover the financial particulars so they were clearly understood.

The suggestion was also made that someone who had a long history with the company should participate in the presentation. That prompted several team members to call out, "Bernie!"

Audrey, playing devil's advocate, asked if Bernie was being suggested to present the financial aspect of the presentation or to be the personification of an experienced employee.

That prompted a sea of raised hands as the majority of the team saw Bernie as a double threat presenter. As the head of financial services he certainly was adept at making clear, concise presentations guaranteed not to put his audience to sleep. And he was probably the best company historian and most committed employee Crown had ever had. If anyone could make our prospective clients believers, Bernie was that person.

A vote was taken and there were no nays and no abstentions. Challenge met!

I went directly to Bernie's office and told him what had just happened at the team meeting. He knew about Joe's hospitalization and was eager to do anything he could to help. He was pleased to be the spontaneous and unanimous choice of the team for such an important role in the presentation. He was eager to be brought up to speed and to do anything he could to help.

My next stop was Russ's office. I briefed him on the presentation plans and explained how we arrived at them. He was as supportive and enthusiastic as Bernie had been.

"I congratulate you, Mike," he said as he stood up, which was my cue not to linger. "You're doing a great job putting this together."

"It's the team that's doing a great job, Russ." "I know. That's why you are being congratulated. You did select the personnel, and made them a team. I know you still have a lot of work ahead of you so I won't take any more of your time right now, but I want you to keep me well informed on your progress as we get closer to the presentation date. And here's something for you."

I took the napkin he handed me and read the quotation as I walked back to my office:

Like every beginner, I have thought you could beat, pummel and thrash an idea into existence.
Under such treatment, of course, any decent idea folds its paws, turns on its back, fixes its eyes on eternity,anddies.

Ray Bradbury

John A. DiCicco and Kenneth E. Strong, Jr.

We Can Fix This

Like every beginner, I have thought you could beat, pummel and thrash an idea into existence.
Under such treatment, of course, any decent idea folds up its paws, turns on its back, fixes its eyes on eternity, and dies.

Ray Bradbury

This is a key rule: create a psychological contract with your subordinate that simply says: Your subordinates will get the credit when things go well and you will take the blame when things go wrong. The main reason why subordinates will not take risks is that they have been hung out to dry when things go wrong or someone else takes the credit when things go right.

To help your subordinates develop their leadership skills to their fullest potential you must delegate duties and assignments in successively greater degrees of complexity. Leaders are developed best through experiential projects or assignments rather than by textbooks and manuals.

As each new assignment is completed on time, but perhaps not perfectly, the level of difficulty must be increased. By adopting this tactic you are clearly communicating the message that your trainees are expected to perform at a high level of effectiveness and to manage their time wisely. Your subordinates must take risks in order to satisfactorily meet your requirements.

The first step is to clearly outline the assignment. Specify time constraints, resources available (this includes you) and what the expected outcome must be for the assignment to be considered a success. Don't forget to allow time for questions. Provide a brief overview of why the assignment is important. Also include who, what and where support and challenges are most likely to be found. Establish a schedule of meetings to monitor progress. These meetings should be no longer than fifteen minutes. Now that you have set your subordinates up for success cut them loose and let them get to it.

Two things can happen when subordinates take risks. One is good and the other is not so good. However, both results have a tremendous impact on the willingness of your leader-in-training to take future risks. The assignment may go well and be completed satisfactorily and on time. When this is the outcome you must make a public acknowledgement of the success and make sure the person in training gets the credit for a successful outcome.

The not so good result is when the assignment does not go well or is completed after the deadline. There may be a number of valid reasons why the outcome was not what was required. The unsuccessful trainee doesn't need to be showered with blame to realize the outcome was unsuccessful. He or she needs to understand why the outcome was unsuccessful so it isn't repeated.

Conduct an after action review to affirm what went well and what went wrong and how this result can be prevented in the future. This process will contribute to the learning experience.

Being blamed or criticized for taking a risk and failing won't stop your subordinates from failing; it will stop them from trying. You must be the person to stop this all too frequent practice of placing blame. Instead, simply approach your subordinate and say, "We can fix this" and begin to assist him or her in taking the necessary steps to correct the assignment by giving practical guidance to prevent a recurrence. If you follow this process faithfully your subordinates will continue to take on more challenging assignments and greater risks.

This practice demonstrates that you mean what you say, you are a person of character, you are making allowances for their professional development experience and you are not going to deliberately let them fail. The result is that you will have an extremely loyal and competent staff whose performance will far exceed that of their contemporaries. Your reputation will spread throughout the organization as a leader's leader who trains future leaders of the organization.

Remember when you adopt the practice of "we can fix this" you turn success into a given when your subordinates are assigned a task.

Chapter Fourteen

Take Action

It was the following day and in a few minutes I was meeting with Audrey and Bernie to get down to the nitty-gritty of the presentation. Some shadowy doubts had crept into my mind and I was trying to evict them.

Yesterday, working with the team and solving our unexpected loss of Joe as our presenter and establishing a plan to replace him, was very satisfying. At the end of the day yesterday, I really felt on top of things.

But now we had to actually commit to the specifics of the presentation. The importance of those decisions, and the possible consequences of making the wrong decisions now seemed overwhelming to me. We couldn't possibly include every single element about the services we would be providing.

As the team leader the ultimate responsibility for the outcome of this project would be mine. I can't know what to include and what to leave out, what to emphasize and what to just touch on. The phrase 'Do something, even if it's wrong' certainly wasn't an option. Wrong is what I have to avoid. But doing nothing is equally unacceptable.

I can't do nothing and I can't do something I know is wrong, so all I can do is make the best decisions possible based on what I do know. As obvious as that conclusion may seem, it took some soul searching to arrive at it, but once I did, those shadowy doubts in my mind vacated the premises and my self-confidence returned.

Audrey and Bernie arrived together, Audrey looking anxious and Bernie looking eager. We seated ourselves at a small table and each poised our pencils over a legal pad. No one spoke for twenty seconds or so until Bernie asked, "Anyone feeling anxious?"

Audrey responded immediately, "Yes, Bernie, how did you know?"

Bernie smiled his slow, warm smile and said, "Well we've been given an important assignment and it's only natural to feel the weight of that responsibility and wonder if we're up to it."

"That's it exactly, Bernie. Do you feel that way?"

"I certainly understand what an important responsibility we've been given, but the people who chose us have as big a stake in this as we do and they believe we can do it."

"And we aren't in this alone, Audrey," I reminded her. "The team has prepared excellent information and they are all available for any backup information, explanation, guidance or any kind of help we may need. It's still a team project and we're not going to let anyone down."

"You know, Audrey," Bernie said, "No one knows everything. We already have a good base of knowledge about this and we'll learn more as we go along. Ultimately we'll have to make the best decisions we can based on the information we have. And if not us, then who?"

"Okay," Audrey said, "Where do we start?" "Let's start with a rough draft, and take it to the team to critique," I suggested.

"That's a good approach, Mike," Bernie said, "How many drafts do you anticipate we will go through to produce the final presentation?"

"I think there will be a great many drafts, Bernie, and I believe that the more there are, the better the final draft will be. My goal is to produce a final draft that everyone on the team approves."

"Do you think that's possible?" Audrey asked.

"I think it's essential. The work of everyone on this team must be represented in the presentation. And they must approve what we include of their work."

"You're going to need some diplomat to manage that, Mike."

"I'm looking at him, Bernie. You have impressive experience with the company, loyalty beyond question and the respect of everyone on the team."

"You can't deny that, Bernie," Audrey said. "The team wanted you for the presentation unanimously."

"Okay, Mike, I'll do my best. And when do you plan to let Russ review a draft?"

"Ideally I'd like to have Russ see the second to the last draft."

"And just how are you going to know when it's the second to the last draft, Mike?"

"I said ideally. It may not work out ideally, but in any event I want him to see a draft before the final draft, but not a draft that involves any serious disagreement."

"I think we should be able to pull that off," Bernie said.

"Good," I said, "Now shall we get started on draft number one?"

We put in four productive hours before a tap on my door made us all look up to see Russ standing there.

"Don't you people have homes?" he asked, in mock surprise. "You're running up the light bill here. Shouldn't you be calling it a night?

Audrey and Bernie gathered their things, said their goodnights and left. Russ looked at the multiple sheets of the presentation outline lying on the table and smiled. "I see you had a productive session," he observed.

"Yes, we did. Bernie and Audrey are great people to work with. I feel very positive about this, Russ."

"Glad to hear that. Not surprised, but glad. I have great confidence in you and your team, Mike. Here, this is for you. See you tomorrow," he said as he handed me a folded napkin and walked out of the office.

I opened the napkin and read the quotation on it.

Anything that we have to learn we learn by the actual doing of it. We become just by performing just acts, temperate by performing temperate ones, brave by performing brave ones.

Aristotle

Take Action

What strikes fear in many leaders is the lack of knowing all the information about the situation when the resulting success or failure of the task assigned or its result places the organization at risk. In such a situation you may be less likely to commit company resources whether it's personnel, money or materials. No one wants to be responsible for making a decision that results in a failed attempt and the consequences that follow.

It's important to remember that you do not make decisions in a vacuum nor do you gather information to make your decisions alone. But you alone take responsibility for the results of the decision. But here's the rub; our culture glorifies winners and ridicules failures.

Everyone loves a winner and who doesn't want to be loved. Nobody wants to be the goat either! Buy you are not paid to be loved; you are paid to make decisions that no one else wants to or has the required skills or aptitude to make because they are afraid to take action.

Don't let the lack of knowledge prevent you from taking action and making your decisions.

Prepare with the information you have at hand and learn the rest of the data, procedures, policies and methods as you go along. The secret is simply to take action. This action orientation is what separates you as a leader from others who are followers.

Use all available resources at your disposal to formulate your plan of action, bring in all the resources at your disposal, get the best advice you can, evaluate the recommendations and make your decision. This is the hard part because your decision is made alone, in the solitude of your mind.

Don't let the fear of failure paralyze your decision- making ability. Take action!

Leaders are known for their good judgment. You learn good judgment through the experience of making mistakes and learning from each mistake. In doing so you build a set of skills that improves your future decision-making success rate.

So get comfortable with it and make your decisions anyway. To become a successful leader you must become action oriented and people will follow. You can do it!

Anything that we have to learn we learn by the actual doing of it. We become just by performing just acts, temperate by performing temperate ones, brave by performing brave ones.

Aristotle

Chapter Fifteen

Better A Guide Than A Coach

In the days that followed, my prediction that there would be multiple drafts of the presentation proved to be accurate. Fortunately, my belief that with each draft the presentation would become better and better was also justified.

Initially representatives of each department sought to protect their vested interests, resisting any efforts to summarize or eliminate any portion of their contribution. While I saw my role at that point as a guide, at times I felt more like a referee.

After several hours of fruitless efforts we broke for lunch. I joined Bernie and Audrey at a small table in the cafeteria and we discussed our options.

"We have adequate time to complete this project, but not if we spend time as unproductively as we did this morning," I said. We made absolutely no progress in more than three hours."

Audrey observed, "I know, Mike but we are dealing with a very intelligent group of people."

"No one questions that, Audrey," Bernie said, "But what's your point?"

"Well after our total lack of progress this morning, it has to have become as obvious to the rest of the team as it has to us that everyone can't have everything they want in the presentation. Every department has to make some compromises."

"And?" Bernie spoke in a questioning tone.

"And," Audrey continued, "it's not a question of deciding if they can make compromises, but what compromises they need to make to strengthen rather than weaken the presentation."

"You're absolutely right, Audrey," I said, "and now I know what we're going to do." Then I explained what I had in mind for the rest of the day.

When we returned to the meeting room you could sense the frustration the team was feeling. When the meeting began that morning they were seated randomly, but now they were sitting in little clusters, by department.

"I know you are all feeling frustrated by our lack of progress this morning. I take note of the fact that you have seated yourselves pretty much by department. Are you preparing for battle?" I asked. This prompted a lot of shuffling and very little eye contact.

"It would be a foolish battle," I continued. "No matter who won, Crown would lose. And all of you *are* Crown. To state the obvious, every department cannot have everything they have compiled included in the presentation. It would be ineffective. It would be a deal killer. We have been asked for a presentation, not a symposium.

"It isn't a question of whether you are going to make some compromises; it's a question of what compromises you are going to make. And I suggest that the criteria should be to eliminate or summarize or otherwise alter the material representative of your department based on strengthening the presentation." I looked over the group and one man made steady eye contact with me, and stood up.

"Could I say something?" he asked.

"Certainly. Speak up. We're a team here."

"Do you have any idea how hard it is, not to include what you consider critical information about your department, information that you believe might help get that contract?"

"Yes, I certainly do. This morning made a real believer of me. But we can't afford any more three-hour meetings with no positive results. You know what you need to do, and since you're already seated by department, I propose that you meet in departmental groups for the balance of the day and come back tomorrow morning with some progress to show one another. Are there any objections to that?" Hearing none, I gathered my notes as the groups began shuffling papers and talking among themselves.

"One last thing," I said, as I paused at the door, "I'm very proud of this group and the progress you have made up to this morning. I know how long and hard you have worked on this project. Pride in and loyalty to your individual departments is a laudable and positive thing, but we can't let something so positive have a negative effect on the company." With that the three of us left and heard the sound of conversations beginning and papers rustling before we had closed the door.

"I think that went very well," Bernie said. "I'll be very surprised if we don't see some significant progress tomorrow."

"Audrey," I said, "You're awfully quiet. Do you have a different take on this?"

"No, not at all," she said with a smile. "They understand what they have to do and why they have to do it, and you acknowledged how difficult it will be for them and how hard they have worked to this point. I think that's just what they needed."

"Then why didn't you tell us that first thing this morning?" Bernie asked.

"Because I didn't realize it then," she answered a little sheepishly.

I parted company with Audrey and Bernie and stopped by the cafeteria for a cup of coffee. I sat at the table mulling over the events of the day when Russ sat down across from me. "You need a jolt of caffeine, Russ?" I asked gesturing toward the coffeemaker and starting to stand up.

"No, thanks, Mike," he said, waving me back to my seat. "I saw you leaving the meeting as I was on my way out. I noticed you, Bernie and Audrey left the team on its own. How did the morning meeting go?"

"Not well would be an understatement. We made absolutely no progress whatsoever. Not one department was willing to give up one word."

"That didn't surprise you, did it?"

"I can't say that I expected it. But I don't think it surprised Audrey. And with some good input from her I think we were able to get the team back on track. I suggested they work in departmental groups the rest of the day and have some results for us in the morning."

"How did they react to that?"

"I could hear conversations beginning and papers rustling as I closed the door, so I'd call their reaction positive."

"And of course you gave them a pat on the back and acknowledged their hard work and the hard work they have ahead of them." Russ made the statement a question by raising his eyebrows.

"Of course," I replied with a hint of a smile.

"Good," he said, as he stood up, "I predict you'll see some good results tomorrow. You have a good team, Mike, and you're handling this well. And here's something for you."

I reached for the napkin before he took it out of his pocket and I could see him chuckling to himself as he left. This was the quotation:

What I hear I forget
What I see I remember
What I do I understand
          Confucius

Better A Guide Than A Coach

What I hear I forget
What I see I remember
What I do I understand
          Confucius

A tremendous amount of discussion and numerous books and articles has been devoted to coaching others, not just in sports but also in the business world.

Coaching has become a buzzword. Rather than supervising, managing, training, counseling or mentoring subordinates, you have become a coach.

It is interesting that as our society becomes less personalized and more technical our language is being modified to lessen the impact of words.

Supervisors, managers, leaders and mentors now become coaches. Are we really evolving into a more participative style of leadership or simply becoming politically correct to soften authoritative words? I am not sure, but I know I don't like it.

My issue with being a coach in the business world is that the executive or managerial coach does not participate in the game, does not go in harm's way and does not take the risks the players do. He or she is confined to the sidelines, watching, not exposed to the danger, failure or mistakes.

I believe coaching is a wonderful educational method but ineffective as a training experience. I define training as the process of teaching the required skills and knowledge for the staff member's current job. The best way to train staff based on that definition is as a guide.

A guide's purpose is to safely navigate the terrain with you from point A to point B. Along the way the guide identifies dominant features of the landscape, such as hazards, safety precautions, alternate routes, how to protect yourself from the weather, rest stops, how to read a map or compass, where to find food and water, the basics of first aid, how to pack your gear and the best vistas to view and enjoy. He or she trains you to navigate the terrain on your own in the future rather than talking you through your journey in the cabin and then sending you on your way.

The guide differs from the coach in this way. At the end of the journey the guide will have transferred knowledge and hands on practice that will enable the student to understand and experience the following: The student will know what is to be accomplished, why the journey is important, when the task is to be accomplished, where the task is to be performed and how to do the task based on knowledge gained from the guide and practical experience.

As you guide staff through the journey, they are drawing

their own conclusions, making mental notes and planning their next journey, using the guide's knowledge and experience as a foundation. The guide is creating an environment where a staff member can come to practice his or her job. A guide draws out of his or her student three key learning styles, visual, audio and kinesthetic: seeing, hearing and doing. Adults learn best by doing.

The guide ensures that there are programmed, confidence building exercises and decision-making points for the student along the journey. The goal is that towards the end of the journey the student becomes the guide ready for his or her own adventures.

John A. DiCicco and Kenneth E. Strong, Jr.

Notes and Action Plan

Chapter Sixteen

Look Beyond Your Tenure

I can't say that the remaining weeks before the presentation were uneventful, but they were without major glitches, unpleasant surprises and, best of all, any team dissention. To a man, and woman, everyone on the team was pleased with the final presentation and no one was more pleased than Russ.

I went to see Joe, who was home recovering, to tell him in person that our presentation had been successful and we had been awarded the contract. Joe came to the door himself and showed me into his family room.

"I hope you're feeling as good as you look, Joe," I said as he gave me a firm handshake and a big grin.

"I feel fine, Mike. The doctor says I can begin the new job in a month barring any complications," he said, sitting down and waving me to a chair. "And I'm sure that Crown got the contract," he added.

"What makes you so sure of that, Joe?" I asked.

"You made me sure. You and your team and the way you went about preparing for the presentation persuaded me. As reluctant as I was originally about presenting all that technical information, you convinced me that I could do it justice with the support of the team. And that's saying something."

"I don't mind telling you, Joe, when I learned that you couldn't do the presentation I was nearly thrown for a loop."

"Mike, I don't think anyone thought that way but you. And I'd say you got over it quite well."

"Well you know Russ. He believes there are only challenges, not problems."

"And I'd say he's made a believer out of you." "Oh I believe in Russ all right, Joe."

"That's not what I meant, Mike. I meant he's made you believe in yourself."

"Yes, he has. He's really quite a remarkable person."

"You know what he would say, if you said that to him? He'd say, 'That's my job.' "

"You're right, Joe," I agreed, "That's just what he'd say."

Joe and I exchanged good wishes for our careers and he sent his regards to everyone at Crown and I headed back to the office for meetings with Audrey and Russ respectively. When I got back to the office I was early for my first meeting so I stopped by the cafeteria for a quick cup of coffee. Audrey was sitting at a table by herself and I joined her.

"How is Joe doing, Mike?"

"Very well, I'm happy to report. And not at all surprised that we got the contract. He had a lot of faith in the team."

"Well I don't think that was the case in the very beginning, Mike."

"No, but we hadn't become a team in the very beginning. But we certainly finished strong. And you played a significant part in that, Audrey."

"Thank you. I really enjoyed being a part of the team."
"Audrey, I've been thinking about the contribution you made

and the way you utilized your skills. I'd like you to continue to work with me on special projects in the future. Would you be interested in that?

"Oh, yes, I certainly would. I know I have a lot to learn, but I work hard and I do learn quickly."

"You don't have to sell me, Audrey," I said with a smile, "I'm already sold." You have a lot to offer this company and I'm confident that there's a bright future for you here."

We finished our coffee and I went to Russ's office for our meeting. Our presentation had been so successful we were going to review the elements and format of the presentation with the intent of creating a format for future presentations.

Russ was on his feet as I got to the door of his office, asking about Joe. I gave him the good news about his condition and got a bit of a smile from him when I told him Joe had been confident that we would be awarded the contract.

"Did he say when he would be able to start the new job?"

"Yes, he said he begins in a month."

"Good, good, I'm glad for Joe. Sit down, Mike and let's review what went right with the presentation. Off the top of my head I can't think of anything that could have been done better, but it's good to go over these things while they're fresh in your mind just in case there is something that could be improved."

We spent over an hour discussing ways the presentation could have been improved. There was a time when I would have considered Russ to be nit picking and taken great exception to the discussion.

But I had come to realize that Russ wasn't second-guessing; he just believed that there is always room for improvement. As we talked I noted where a few small changes should be made, Russ agreed and we incorporated them. Russ never scheduled meetings without a specific purpose. He had made no suggestions because his presence was simply to make this an official meeting, which meant that I had better produce some results. He knew that a scheduled meeting with him would prompt me to carefully review the presentation rather than continue to bask in its success.

"Mike, what do you consider the most important things you've learned from heading up this project?"

"I really don't know where to start, Russ. For one thing I learned that mistakes can be fixed; you don't throw in the towel at the first glitch. But the most important thing I've learned, or maybe relearned, is that leadership and success are all about people. The way the team responded to the challenge they were given is something I'll never forget."

"That's right on, Mike. It is all about people. And that's what leadership is all about, identifying quality people, giving them the opportunity and experience to create and develop to continue to make the company successful. The best leaders identify and mentor potential leaders. A leader's most important legacy is the leaders he or she develops."

"I appreciate all the help you've given me, Russ."

"That's my job, Mike," he said, getting to his feet to indicate the meeting was over, "and it's one of the most rewarding parts of my job."

As I stood up I said, "Russ I'm having a little get-together for the team at lunch tomorrow to thank them and congratulate them and I'd like to tell them about the few changes we decided on, to keep them in the picture. I'd like you to come."

"Be glad to, Mike, and that's a good idea." He reached in his pocket and took out a small napkin, laid it on my desk, shook my hand and left the office. The quotation was:

A leader's greatest success is developing new leaders who ultimately outperform him.

Russell Jacobs

Look Beyond Your Tenure

A leader's greatest success is developing new leaders who ultimately outperform him.

Russell Jacobs

As you are building your career and reputation the last thing on your mind is preparing someone to take your place. But you must plan for this eventuality with as much thoughtfulness as you plan your annual budget or a new project.

The future seems so far away from our day-to-day duties, yet preparing for tomorrow is a principal responsibility of our leadership role. Who will replace us becomes the hardest question of all. This question must be wrestled with without bias on your part. Of course no one can do your job as well as you can, you're not retiring, you're in good health so why think about a succession plan?

Developing your succession plan should be high on your priority list. The dream job that you always wanted may come along suddenly and if you've spent considerable time developing potential replacements you'll feel good about accepting it in a timely fashion and leaving your facility in good hands.

Imagine that you get a call from a recruiter with the opportunity of a lifetime. How can you accept the offer in good conscience when you have not prepared a replacement for your position? How will your company fare after your departure without an experienced and trained replacement?

You must begin to think of your replacement from day one. You will be free to move on quickly without the company asking you to stay until a new replacement can be trained.

Your facility is an ongoing business; the loss of a key person can be crippling for a period of time. As the incumbent you must not put the facility in this situation. With a ready and able replacement you can avoid it.

We are in leadership positions because we demonstrate good judgment. The question becomes, how do you develop good judgment? I believe the most effective way to develop good judgment is through experience and you get experience by performing new assignments and making mistakes.

To develop subordinates for leadership responsibilities and or as your replacement, it is critical to create an environment that allows for mistakes as part of the learning process. I remember when I was a young administrator my father would tell me, "If you're not making any mistakes, you're not doing anything."

Create an environment where mistakes are considered a normal occurrence. You may want to publicly proclaim, "You will make mistakes, but learn from them."

Your business can't grow and develop without taking risks

and when risks are taken mistakes become part of the process. Do everything you can to eliminate the fear of making mistakes.

If you want staff to make ten decisions and seven are mistakes, the benefit of the correct (good judgment) will outweigh the mistakes. The mistake is simply a cost of doing business. Whether a mistake or good judgment is the result the follow up question should be, "So, what have you learned?" The development of a successor is up to you. I believe it is time well spent.

Your business will continue to be successful in part because of your efforts. What better legacy to leave behind than a replacement who will continue the success you helped to create?

John A. DiCicco and Kenneth E. Strong, Jr.

Notes and Action Plan

Chapter Seventeen

Paint Your Own Future

As we come to the end of our leadership journey, I would like to share some final thoughts with you about growing as a leader.

Leadership is about building positive relationships with the people you work with. It does not require a formal title, an advanced degree or a special parking place.

It does require a total commitment to the success of the people who work on your team beyond your self-interest.

BE — KNOW — DO should be posted in a visible location and reviewed daily.

BE demands that you become and remain a person of character who lives by a high standard of values and ethics that blend with your organizational values and ethics.

You must also become a teacher of your organizational values and ethics. Simply put, you walk the talk, setting an example for everyone to follow.

KNOW — People will not follow you unless they are confident that you know what you are doing. It also requires you to maintain your proficiencies in the following areas:

Technical skills, which are your job related skills; conceptual skills, the ability to reason, think and make sound judgments and interpersonal skills, which include teaching, counseling, motivating, coaching and feedback.

Good leaders add to their knowledge and skills every day. You've heard the term life long learning; embrace it and make it part of your personal and professional development plan.

Keeping your skills current and developing new skills equals job security. What this means to you is to pay attention to what is going on around you. Assessing your current skills and blending them with the future skills you will need must be a life long process.

DO — As a leader you are action oriented in three areas:

Influencing others through communication

A leader's need to receive information and gain an understanding of that information is equally as important as giving information.

Motivation of others

The people you lead must have a clear understanding of the organization's challenges and the need to respond to those challenges. Your best motivation tool is recognition of individual efforts.

Positive Attitude

When the going gets tough and chaos reigns, the good leader offers the team a calm center and a source of strength, hope and confidence. A good leader becomes that center of hope and confidence, inspiring employees to believe that no matter what, it will all work out.

Remember that leadership is influencing people by providing purpose, direction and motivation to accomplish the mission and improve the organization.

Make it a commitment to study and practice so that you'll have the skills to BE of good character.

KNOW your job and your people.

Then act, DO what is right to achieve successful assignment results on time, on budget and according to standards.

Leadership is not about positions or titles. It's about behavior. So become a student of human behavior to understand why people do the things they do.

Here are some brief definitions of some behavioral theories. Learning more about them could increase your success in dealing with people.

Attribution Theory

Subconsciously making inferences and judgments about the causes of people's behavior.

Expectancy Theory

Makes the assumption that human beings will choose to engage in behaviors that they believe will lead to the rewards they want.

Equity Theory

Makes the observation that human beings frequently compare their own skills, talents and efforts with those of other people.

Goal Setting Theory

As Lewis Carroll's Cheshire cat said, "If you don't know where you are going, any road will take you there." Successful people are goal-oriented.

Motivation Through Consequences Theory

When behavior in a particular situation is followed by satisfaction, the satisfaction, when the situation recurs, will become associated with that situation and the behavior is also likely to reappear. In contrast any behavior that produces discomfort in a particular situation is less likely to reappear when the situation recurs.

Good leaders must also be good followers. It is important to remember that even when you are identified as a leader, you often hold a complementary role as a follower. Most of us will spend more time as followers than as leaders and it is not uncommon to switch between being a leader and being a follower several times over the course of any given day. Put as much effort and skill into being an exceptional follower as you do in being an exceptional leader.

As a leader the challenges you face will be many and varied. Everything you have learned, heard in passing, seen on TV, read in a newspaper or journal or learned at a conference will be used in your journey as a leader. Everything you have learned in your life will be beneficial to your decision making process.

Understanding your world and your industry are not mutually exclusive, rather they are interrelated. In many ways you must become a modern day renaissance man or woman. Look for new trends, breakthroughs or other opportunities that will increase your value to the organization.

A major portion of each leader's job is to identify and solve problems that affect his or her department. The leader's thought process will help you use behavioral science theories, your experience and your personnel to do the following:

Step 1: Identify what is happening

Step 2: Account for what is happening

Step 3: Take actions to influence what is happening

Step 4: Assess your leadership actions to determine how successful you were

Never forget to celebrate individual and team success. Recognition readily translates into motivation.

Continue your study of leadership to more fully understand your experiences and apply them to future challenges with a clear vision of what needs to be accomplished.

You may be wondering how things worked out for Mike Berber. He got that promotion and others after that, but his greatest satisfaction has been his development of new leaders. As Russ said, that is a leader's greatest success.

And what about you? Are you going to be the Mike Berber at the beginning of our journey or the Mike Berber at the end of our journey?

The Choice Is Yours.

CPSIA information can be obtained
at www.ICGtesting.com
Printed in the USA
LVHW081415150520
655682LV00019B/1454